Rapture 911

What To Do If You're Left Behind

Pocket Edition

Rapture 911
What To Do If You're Left Behind
Pocket Edition

Published by Drezhn Publishing LLC
PO BOX 67458
Albuquerque, NM 87193-7458

Cover design by Dan Van Oss, CoverMint
www.covermint.design

Print Edition – April 2020
Second Edition

ISBN 978-1-947328-36-5

Table Of Contents

WHAT TO DO IF YOU'RE LEFT BEHIND

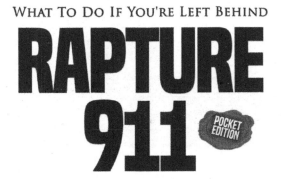

MARSHA KUHNLEY

Introduction

We Have A Rapture Emergency

We have a rapture emergency on our hands. The day is quickly approaching in which Jesus will rapture or take away those who believe in him. I refer to these soon to be raptured people as believers throughout this book. The *rapture* is an imminent event which means it doesn't require any other events to happen first. We're in a state of emergency because the rapture will be a world-changing event and the vast majority of people aren't prepared for it.

There are many types of people who aren't prepared today: people who don't know Jesus or the events that are on the horizon, believers who haven't been taught about the rapture, believers who aren't watching or paying attention for this event, believers who know it's coming but have a blasé attitude about it, and then we have the scoffers who mock the rapture. The scoffers could be believers or unbelievers. We also mustn't forget about the believers who know the rapture is coming and who want people they care about to know about it, get saved, and not be left behind.

People who live in areas prone to natural disasters like earthquakes, tornadoes, hurricanes, and tsunamis are typically prepared for those events. They have emergency supplies on hand, a place to shelter, an evacuation plan, etc. When a hurricane is forming, weather forecasters give us a heads-up on where the storm is going to make landfall and how bad it's going to be. People in the area then prepare. They board up their homes, get supplies, go to a shelter, or evacuate if needed. If you lived in an area like this and had been told ahead of time that a disaster was coming, you'd prepare for it.

Yet there's a world changing event on the horizon that we know could happen any minute and we're not prepared for it. We can and should be prepared. God has told us to pay attention and watch for this event. For the people left behind after the rapture, they must deal with a magnitude of horror that none of us can possibly imagine. Let that sink in for a minute. No natural disaster that has ever happened will compare to what's coming. None of them.

If you're a believer, you likely have someone in your life who you care about who doesn't have a relationship with Jesus. If the rapture happened this very next second, that person would be left behind. In that moment of time, God removed the believers who were the only light in a very dark world. How dark it will be that day. Now what are those people you care about going to do? They won't have you to tell them what happened and where everyone disappeared to because you got raptured. In fact, they won't have any believer who had a real relationship with Jesus around who they can turn to for help. They'll all be gone. Sure, there'll be some people left behind who claim to be Christians, but they never accepted Jesus into their hearts. Otherwise, they would have been raptured too. While some of those people will immediately understand what's happened and why they got left behind, the vast majority won't. So the only people who will be left behind who will be providing answers to the people you care about are people who don't know the truth, who don't believe, and most who frankly don't want to ever believe. The world leaders will be spewing all sorts of lies.

That's the emergency. The people who will be left behind won't be prepared. After the rapture, they'll need a resource they can go to for quick answers about what happened and why and what they need to do to be saved. Yes, they'll find the answers in the Bible, but they won't know that. Who's going to tell them that? If they're smart enough to seek answers in the Bible, they won't know how to read the Bible or where to even look for answers. That's what this book is for: to help those who will be left behind. Hopefully every single one of them who reads this book will come to believe in Jesus and be saved.

Reader Who Is Left Behind

Dear Reader,

I'm so sorry you're left behind. You need to know that God loves you. I know it doesn't seem like it right now, but he does. In fact, he loves you unconditionally. It doesn't matter what you've done in your past or what you'll do in your future. He loves you regardless. He loves you even though he left you behind. You also need to know that you haven't missed your chance to be saved, to spend eternity with God in heaven, and to reunite with the people you care about who were raptured.

God put a burden on my heart to write this book just for you. He wanted to make sure you had a resource where you could find truthful answers quickly. This is because you're going to be bombarded with every lie and deceit imaginable by your leaders, the media, scientists, scholars, your friends, everyone. You see, God wants you to know the truth about what happened and why. He wants you to come to know him and put your faith in him. It's not too late, but it will be very soon.

I'm so excited that you're starting your faith journey. You're going to learn a lot and you're going to be confronted with some difficult truths. However, if you stick with reading this resource, you're going to come out on the other side with the ability to cope with what's happened and be well prepared for what's to come. And I'm hoping you make the choice to put your faith in Jesus. If you do, then look me up when you get to heaven or when you enter the millennial kingdom. I'd love to hear your story and how you overcame.

God is with you on your journey.

Reader Who Is A Believer

Dear Reader,

As a believer, you have the power to make a difference in this emergency. You can help those who will be left behind. You can put this book and a Bible in a place someone you care about would find if they came looking for you after the rapture.

But you know what, if you're reading this that means the rapture hasn't happened yet. So better yet, you can read this book and educate yourself about the rapture and future events so that you can have a conversation with the people you care about. Hopefully they'll come to believe in Jesus before the rapture and won't be left behind. The other thing you can do now is give this book and a Bible to the people you care about as a reference. I know what you're thinking: They'll think I'm crazy if I give them a rapture survival book! Maybe, but it would be worth it for them to know the truth wouldn't it? Don't be embarrassed or ashamed to share God's truth with someone. Those emotions are just scare tactics from Satan. Remember that we're in a war, and he doesn't want you saving anyone. Where would you be today if no one had the guts to share the truth with you?

I want to make sure there's information for people who are left behind that will help them come to learn the truth and have a relationship with Jesus, just like you and I do. Join me in this war, and let's go rescue some souls!

Reader Who Is Curious Or Was Given This Book

Dear Reader,

So you're curious about the rapture and what the emergency is all about? Or maybe you're here because a Christian who cares about you gave you this book and you thought you'd crack it open and see what's inside? I'm excited that you're here.

I want you to know that you don't have to be left behind when the rapture happens. The choice is still yours to make. The rapture could happen any moment though, so don't put off making the choice. Not making a choice to believe in Jesus is actually making a choice to not believe. You're either with him or against him, there's no neutral zone. If you don't choose to follow Jesus and the rapture happens, you'll be left behind. In this book you're going to learn all about the rapture, why it's going to happen, and how you can be saved from it.

God loves you and is with you in your quest to know him. I'm praying that you come to put your faith in the one he sent to save your soul—Jesus.

Tips For Reading This Book

You can read this book from cover to cover like a traditional book, or you can read it like a reference book and go straight to a chapter of interest.

I've written the book with a unique perspective. It's written with the assumption that the person reading it is one of the left behind and that the rapture has already happened. If you are reading this book prior to the rapture, please keep this in mind.

I've included a lot of Scripture in this book because above all else, I want you to know the truth. If you're reading this after the rapture has happened, it will be hard for you to find a Bible. That's because your enemy, Satan, wants you blinded to the truth and deceived. Bibles will quickly become a scarce commodity, so I've included the actual Scriptures in this book that I'll be explaining.

Scripture references in this book come from the World English Bible (WEBP), unless otherwise noted. This translation of the Bible is in the public domain and free to read. It uses modern English, and it's easy to read. It's based on the American Standard Version of the Bible that was published in 1901, the Biblia Hebraica Stutgartensa Old Testament, and the Greek Majority Text New Testament. You can visit my website or the World English Bible website to read or download a free copy of this Bible.

Rapture911.com

WorldEnglishBible.org

As you read this book, I know you'll gain a better understanding of God's word, and the truth will be revealed to you. On your quest for truth, I encourage you to discover and read God's word for yourself and test all that I have told you. In the Scripture I've included below, you'll see this is exactly what the Bereans did when they were visited by the apostle Paul. They examined God's word for themselves to make sure what they were being taught was legitimate.

> The brothers immediately sent Paul and Silas away by night to Beroea. When they arrived, they went into the Jewish synagogue. Now these were more noble than those in Thessalonica, in that they received the word with all readiness of mind, examining the Scriptures daily to see whether these things were so. (Acts 17:10-11)

After each Scripture I've included, you'll see a reference for where it came from in parentheses like this: (Acts 17:10-11). That means the verses are from the Bible, the book of Acts, chapter 17, verses 10 and 11. All Bibles will have the books clearly labeled and the chapters and verses clearly numbered. Sometimes in this book you'll see Scripture references with an additional descriptor like (Acts 17:10-11 NIV). The extra NIV refers to the Bible version the Scripture came from. Instead of the WEBP, I used the NIV. I've typically done this because I preferred the word choice and grammar of that particular translation. I knew it would be easier for you to understand.

If you haven't read the Bible before, take a look at Chapter 15 - How To Read The Bible.

Before you continue reading, I recommend you say a simple prayer to God. I've included a prayer at the end of this section that you can use. You need to pray first because Satan, who is currently the "god of this world," the earth, doesn't want you reading this book or understanding anything in it. He's blinded you and you need God's help to overcome this.

> The god of this world has blinded the minds of the unbelieving, that the light of the Good News of the glory of Christ, who is the image of God, should not dawn on them. (2 Corinthians 4:4)

This prayer below will tell God that you are serious about learning the truth and need his help to be successful. Now a prayer is just talking to God. You can pray out loud or silently, whichever you prefer. Prayer is very powerful when you approach God with a sincere heart. He will listen and respond to you.

"God, I pray that you help me read and understand what's written in this book and in particular the Bible verses. I come to you with a heart that's open to learning the truth. I also ask for your love and comfort as I'm confronted with truths that will be difficult for me to hear."

Part 1
Quick Truths

Chapter 1 - What Happened

Millions of people from all across the planet have vanished. It's an event we've referred to as the rapture. The word *rapture* means to be seized, carried off, snatched away, or taken to another place of existence. You won't find the word *rapture* in most Bible translations. Instead you'll likely find the phrase "caught up." In Latin the word for "caught up" is *rapio* and is where we get the English word *rapture*.

Here's one of the rapture passages from the Bible that explains what happened. There are many others that I'll go over in detail later in this book.

> But we don't want you to be ignorant, brothers, concerning those who have fallen asleep, so that you don't grieve like the rest, who have no hope. For if we believe that Jesus died and rose again, even so God will bring with him those who have fallen asleep in Jesus. For this we tell you by the word of the Lord, that we who are alive, who are left until the coming of the Lord, will in no way precede those who have fallen asleep. For the Lord himself will descend from heaven with a shout, with the voice of the archangel and with God's trumpet. The dead in Christ will rise first, then we who are alive, who are left, will be caught up together with them in the clouds, to meet the Lord in the air. So we will be with the Lord forever. Therefore comfort one another with these words. (1 Thessalonians 4:13-18)

This passage tells us that Jesus, "the Lord," gathered all the people who believed he died and rose again. These people were the believers. He gathered two groups of believers. First, those who believed and were already dead which you read as "dead in Christ" and "fallen asleep in Jesus." Second, those who believed and were still alive. He met them all in the clouds. Now all those people will be with Jesus forever.

In the rapture, God took the people who placed their faith in his son Jesus up to heaven. This is God's greatest promise. If you believe in Jesus, you get eternal life.

> For God so loved the world, that he gave his one and only Son, that whoever believes in him should not perish, but have eternal life. (John 3:16)

So what exactly did the raptured people believe about Jesus? They believed that God sent his son Jesus to die for their sins. They also believed that Jesus didn't stay dead; that he rose from the grave and proved he was God in the flesh.

> For I delivered to you first of all that which I also received: that Christ died for our sins according to the Scriptures, that he was buried, that he was raised on the third day according to the Scriptures. (1 Corinthians 15:3-4)

You see, we've all sinned, and we all deserve death and an eternal life separated from God because of that. This Scripture further expounds upon the great news. God redeemed us with the blood of Jesus. The people who were raptured understood that when you place your faith in what Jesus did, God considers you righteous.

> But now apart from the law, a righteousness of God has been revealed, being testified by the law and the prophets; even the righteousness of God through faith in Jesus Christ to all and on all those who believe. For there is no distinction, for all have sinned, and fall short of the glory of God; being justified freely by his grace through the

redemption that is in Christ Jesus, whom God sent to be an atoning sacrifice through faith in his blood, for a demonstration of his righteousness through the passing over of prior sins, in God's forbearance; to demonstrate his righteousness at this present time, that he might himself be just and the justifier of him who has faith in Jesus. (Romans 3:21-26)

Chapter 2 - Why It Happened

The rapture happened for a number of reasons. Here are a few to help you get a quick understanding. I'll explain in great detail later in this book.

God removed the believers from earth because God's wrath has come. I think many of you know the history of Noah and the flood. God told Noah to build an ark because a flood was coming. The flood was God's wrath because the world had become so wicked and filled with violence. Noah was protected from that wrath in the ark. The rapture is a similar type of event.

> God said to Noah, "I will bring an end to all flesh, for the earth is filled with violence through them. Behold, I will destroy them and the earth. Make a ship of gopher wood. ... I, even I, will bring the flood of waters on this earth, to destroy all flesh having the breath of life from under the sky. Everything that is in the earth will die. But I will establish my covenant with you. You shall come into the ship, you, your sons, your wife, and your sons' wives with you." (Genesis 6:13-14, 17-18)

God's wrath is not meant for believers. Noah was protected from it and the people who were raptured are now being protected from it. In these two verses, "us" refers to the believers; people who placed their faith in Jesus.

> Jesus, who delivers us from the wrath to come. (1 Thessalonians 1:10)

> For God didn't appoint us to wrath, but to the obtaining of salvation through our Lord Jesus Christ. (1 Thessalonians 5:9)

Another reason the rapture happened is because God wants everyone to be saved.

> God our Savior, who desires all people to be

saved and come to full knowledge of the truth. (1 Timothy 2:3-4)

God created every one of you reading this. He loves you. He wants you to live with him in eternity in heaven. If you're reading this after the rapture and you are one of the left behind, I know it probably doesn't feel like God loves you right now. Know that he most certainly does. These Scriptures tell us that God loves us so much that he sent his son Jesus to die for us. In fact, he sent Jesus to die for you thousands of years ago, knowing you were going to be a sinner. God didn't show this act of love for you once you cleaned up your life, didn't sin as much, started going to church, etc. Nope. That's because God's love is unconditional.

> By this God's love was revealed in us, that God has sent his one and only Son into the world that we might live through him. In this is love, not that we loved God, but that he loved us, and sent his Son as the atoning sacrifice for our sins. ... We love him, because he first loved us. (1 John 4:9-10, 19)

> But God commends his own love toward us, in that while we were yet sinners, Christ died for us. (Romans 5:8)

God often uses things we perceive as bad like pain, sorrow, sickness, death, and loss in order to bring us closer to him. This is a time of testing for you. The rapture will help many people realize God exists. The Bible tells us that many, many people will become believers through the coming events. Don't waste the opportunity. This is your last chance to place your faith in Jesus and be saved.

> Yahweh your God is testing you, to know whether you love Yahweh your God with all your heart and with all your soul. (Deuteronomy 13:3)

Yahweh is a term used in the Old Testament books

of the Bible and it refers to God's proper name. It's often translated LORD or God. That Scripture told us why God tests us. It's so he can tell if you love him with all your heart. As one of the left behind, how you handle what's to come will reveal your attitude toward God. This time of testing will be difficult for you; don't give up. If you decide to place your faith in Jesus, everything will work out for your good.

> My son, don't take lightly the chastening of the Lord, nor faint when you are reproved by him; for whom the Lord loves, he disciplines, and chastises every son whom he receives. (Hebrews 12:5-6)

> We know that all things work together for good for those who love God, for those who are called according to his purpose. (Romans 8:28)

Another purpose for the rapture is to usher in God's time of wrath against the wicked, just like the flood in Noah's day punished the wicked. The rapture and the events that happen during the tribulation period will do the same. Now, if you have a bad attitude toward God about the situation you're in as one of the left behind, and you get bitter and angry and shake your fist at God in defiance, well you're going to experience his wrath.

> According to your hardness and unrepentant heart you are treasuring up for yourself wrath in the day of wrath ... God; who "will pay back to everyone according to their works:" ... to those who are self-seeking, and don't obey the truth, but obey unrighteousness, will be wrath, indignation, oppression, and anguish on every soul of man who does evil. (Romans 2:5-6, 8-9)

Chapter 3 - Deception Warning

One of the first things that's going to happen after the rapture is strong delusion. *Delusion* means a false belief or to mislead. *Delusion* is an attack on the truth. We can already see this in the world today. With so much fake news and deception, it's often quite difficult to determine what the truth is. It will get way worse after the rapture.

It's going to get worse because God is going to let everyone left behind believe Satan's lies. Satan is "the lawless one." This deception and "working of error" is meant to test everyone's heart. It'll harden the hearts of and further blind people who don't want anything to do with God.

> Then the lawless one will be revealed ... and with all deception of wickedness for those who are being lost, because they didn't receive the love of the truth, that they might be saved. Because of this, God sends them a working of error, that they should believe a lie; that they all might be judged who didn't believe the truth, but had pleasure in unrighteousness. (2 Thessalonians 2:8, 10-12)

So what is truth? God and his word are truth. God is perfect and holy and can't lie. The Bible is his word; God's Spirit was with every one of the authors as they wrote his words down; God's Spirit was with the scholars as they decided what books to include in the Bible we know today.

> All of your words are truth. Every one of your righteous ordinances endures forever. (Psalm 119:160)

> God, who can't lie. (Titus 1:2)

> Every Scripture is God-breathed and profitable for teaching, for reproof, for correction, and for

instruction in righteousness, that each person who belongs to God may be complete, thoroughly equipped for every good work. (2 Timothy 3:16-17)

As you read this book, you'll learn that Satan is behind every lie and deception. Satan is a creation of God; a fallen angel. The Bible calls him the father of lies and a murderer.

> You are of your father, the devil, and you want to do the desires of your father. He was a murderer from the beginning, and doesn't stand in the truth, because there is no truth in him. When he speaks a lie, he speaks on his own; for he is a liar, and the father of lies. (John 8:44)

Your battle on this earth is not against mankind; it's against Satan and his army of fallen angels. The "principalities, powers, rulers of the darkness," and "spiritual forces of wickedness" describe the demonic angels and their hierarchy.

> For our wrestling is not against flesh and blood, but against the principalities, against the powers, against the world's rulers of the darkness of this age, and against the spiritual forces of wickedness in the heavenly places. (Ephesians 6:12)

To understand the deceptions Satan will use, you need to understand what his goals are. Satan, the "shining one," wants to be God.

> How you have fallen from heaven, shining one, son of the dawn! How you are cut down to the ground, who laid the nations low! You said in your heart, "I will ascend into heaven! I will exalt my throne above the stars of God! I will sit on the mountain of assembly, in the far north! I will ascend above the heights of the clouds! I will make myself like the Most High!" (Isaiah 14:12-14)

He wants to be worshiped just like God, and he wants to create just like God creates. Satan hates God and everything God created. Thus Satan hates you. Satan will lie about God, the Bible, Jesus, Christians, the rapture—anything and everything to do with God. Since Satan wants to be God, he'll try to convince you that he is. The Bible tells us he'll be able to perform all sorts of signs and wonders.

Chapter 4 - You Can Still Be Saved

If you're left behind, you may be thinking you messed up and missed your chance to live in heaven for eternity with God. That's not the case. There's still hope for you. You can be saved too. You can see your loved ones who vanished in the rapture again. The decision is entirely up to you. You just have to make the right choice.

God loves you and wants to spend eternity with you. But there's a problem, and it's called sin. Sin is doing and even thinking anything that isn't perfect and holy. Every single one of us commits sin. We can't help it; it's our nature. It doesn't matter what your sin is or how big or little you perceive your sin to be. It could be lying, lust, pride, or murder. Any sin is sin in God's eyes.

> There is no one who does good, no, not so much as one. (Romans 3:12)

God is perfect and sinless and righteous in every way. Thus so is where he lives, heaven. Sin is the opposite of God. Sin cannot exist in heaven. Since people are inherently sinful, no one can live with God unless the sin problem is taken care of first.

Case in point: Adam and Eve. They lived in the garden of Eden with God. They saw God every day. Heaven is wherever God is, so they essentially lived in heaven. After they sinned and ate from the forbidden tree, they got kicked out of the garden. They couldn't live with God anymore. This Scripture records that event. God sent "him," which is Adam, out from the garden.

> God sent him out from the garden of Eden, to till the ground from which he was taken. So he drove out the man; and he placed cherubim at the east of the garden of Eden, and a flaming sword which turned every way, to guard the way to the tree of life. (Genesis 3:23-24)

Here's the good news: God has a solution for the sin problem. He demands a perfect and spotless sacrifice to atone for sin. When Adam and Eve first sinned, God killed an animal to clothe them and atone for their sin.

> Yahweh God made garments of animal skins for Adam and for his wife, and clothed them. (Genesis 3:21)

In the Old Testament times before Jesus came, God's people sacrificed animals to atone for their sin.

> If anyone of the common people sins unwittingly, in doing any of the things which Yahweh has commanded not to be done, and is guilty, if his sin which he has sinned is made known to him, then he shall bring for his offering a goat, a female without defect, for his sin which he has sinned. He shall lay his hand on the head of the sin offering, and kill the sin offering in the place of burnt offering. (Leviticus 4:27-29)

> Under the old system, the high priest brought the blood of animals into the Holy Place as a sacrifice for sin, and the bodies of the animals were burned outside the camp. (Hebrews 13:11 NLT)

Don't run off to find an animal you can sacrifice to atone for your sin. God's already taken care of the sacrifice offering permanently for you. He loves you so much that he sent Jesus, his perfect and sinless and righteous son, down to earth to live as a man. Jesus was then sacrificed for you. He was crucified to atone for your sin. We know this worked, because Jesus isn't dead. God raised him from the dead. Then Jesus appeared to hundreds of people in his risen state. All you have to do now is believe.

> For God so loved the world, that he gave his one and only Son, that whoever believes in him should

not perish, but have eternal life. (John 3:16)

Belief. It seems too simple doesn't it? But that's the irony, it's not simple at all. In fact, belief is really hard. The Bible says the path to God is narrow and most don't find it. That's because we're accustomed to striving for what we want down here on earth. The harder we work, the more we get. We love to boast about our accomplishments. We love to be in control. That's not God's way. God is in control, and it's about what God did, not what you've done. His solution is a gift. He gave his son as a gift to you. You just have to accept it.

> But God, being rich in mercy, for his great love with which he loved us, even when we were dead through our trespasses, made us alive together with Christ—by grace you have been saved—… for by grace you have been saved through faith, and that not of yourselves; it is the gift of God. (Ephesians 2:4-5, 8)

> For by grace you have been saved through faith, and that not of yourselves; it is the gift of God, not of works, that no one would boast. (Ephesians 2:8-9)

You see, it's God's grace that saved you. As sinners, we are doomed to an eternal life far removed from God. That's God's rule. Grace is God demonstrating his love for us by pardoning us based on us believing Jesus died for our sins. God treated Jesus the way we deserve to be treated. Jesus was crucified. God did that so he could treat us the way Jesus deserves to be treated. Jesus is now in heaven with God.

A person who believes what they cannot yet see has faith. They believe God and that Jesus died for their sins. Have faith.

> Now faith is assurance of things hoped for, proof of things not seen. (Hebrews 11:1)

Here's what you must come to believe.

You recognize that you are a sinner.

You don't want to be a sinner anymore. You ask God to forgive you.

You want to live with God for eternity in heaven.

You know that you can't save yourself.

You believe that God sent his son Jesus to atone for your sin by dying on the cross.

You believe that God raised Jesus from the dead and that Jesus reigns with God in heaven.

You surrender your salvation to Jesus and ask him to come into your life.

Now you can't just go through the motions and say these things. You have to actually mean them, deep down from your heart. That's what faith is all about.

This is the good news of the Bible. That Jesus, the son of God, died for your sins, rose from the grave, and reigns from heaven with God.

> Now I declare to you, brothers, the Good News which I preached to you, which also you received, in which you also stand, by which also you are saved, if you hold firmly the word which I preached to you—unless you believed in vain. For I delivered to you first of all that which I also received: that Christ died for our sins according to the Scriptures, that he was buried, that he was raised on the third day according to the Scriptures. (1 Corinthians 15:1-4)

If you truly believe all those things, then tell God. That's what praying is, just talking to God. Tell him you believe each of those truths and ask him to come into your life. And he will indeed!

> It will be that whoever will call on the name of the Lord will be saved. (Acts 2:21)

> "For I know the thoughts that I think toward you," says Yahweh, "thoughts of peace, and not

of evil, to give you hope and a future. You shall call on me, and you shall go and pray to me, and I will listen to you. You shall seek me, and find me, when you search for me with all your heart." (Jeremiah 29:11-13)

Here's an example prayer you can say to God:

"Lord Jesus, I know that I'm a sinner and that I need your forgiveness so that I can live with you for eternity in heaven. Please forgive me. I believe that you are the son of God and that you died on the cross for my sins. I believe that you rose from the grave! I want to turn from my sins and trust and follow you as Lord and Savior. Please come into my heart and life. In Jesus's name, amen."

Chapter 5 - Left Behind Starter Checklist

Here's a short checklist to help you get through what's happened and prepare for what's to come. A more detailed checklist is included in Chapter 20.

1. Choose to believe that Jesus died for you

This is the most important thing on this checklist. In fact, it's the only thing on this list that matters at all. If you decide not to believe in Jesus, then nothing else is going to make any difference whatsoever. I know that's hard to hear for some of you, but it's the truth. You must choose to believe if you want to be saved and live with God in heaven for eternity.

If you're not ready to make this decision yet, keep reading this book and start on the second item in this checklist. You'll keep learning about God and how much he loves you, and you'll be better equipped to make this decision.

If the rapture has happened, you are now living in very perilous times. Realize you could die at any second regardless of if you believe or not. Your survival during this time isn't guaranteed. It's imperative you make the right choice quickly.

2. Get a Bible

You need to know the truth, and the truth is God's word. So go get a Bible. Truth will be hard to come by; remember that strong delusion is coming. I recommend you get more than one Bible because I think you'll need them. Also get Bibles in multiple formats like a book, an epub or pdf file, and an audio file. Once you have a Bible, you need to actually read it if you want to know the truth. I recommend reading the books of John and Luke first.

3. Get some Bible study resources

I cannot emphasize how important knowing the truth, God's word, is going to be. You'll need to study the Bible, understand what it says, and know how to apply it to your life. I recommend you get a study Bible. These include additional information and commentary to help you understand key verses. You should also look online for teachings and sermons from good preachers and download them. These may be hard for you to find, so here's an idea: if any of your neighbors, friends, or family vanished, they likely had a Bible and may have other resources too.

4. Pray

Talk to God. Tell him what you're going through, how you feel, and what you need. He knows all of that already, but he wants you to have a relationship with him. If you give your burdens to God, he'll give you peace in return.

> The peace of God, which surpasses all understanding, will guard your hearts and your thoughts in Christ Jesus. (Philippians 4:7)

5. Get survival gear

You are now living in dangerous times. Survival skills are essential. You should get some books on prepping and survival and stock up on the supplies they suggest. Or find some old episodes of survival TV shows online and watch them. Focus on the basics: food and water, shelter, and clothing.

6. Stick together

It's very difficult to be alone and survive in perilous conditions. Two people will come up with more ideas and be able to tackle more problems than a single person. Find a friend or group of people that you can get through this difficult time with. Then stick together and support each other.

Check out my website, rapture911.com, for links to resources.

Part 2
The Rapture And Why It Happened

Chapter 6 - The Rapture

The rapture is an event the Bible tells us happens in the last days before the second coming of Jesus. The word *rapture* means to be caught up, snatched away, seized, or carried off to another place of existence. That's exactly what happened to the millions of people who disappeared. Jesus took them to heaven. I like to think of it like the Star Trek teleportation technology. Jesus "beamed up" all those people who disappeared.

The millions of people who disappeared may not appear to have anything in common. They'll be from all over the planet and be of different races, genders, ages, incomes, and cultures. However, they did have one very important belief in common. Each person who disappeared had put their faith in Jesus Christ. Throughout this book I will refer to these people as believers.

Some of you may wonder who this Jesus is, why someone would put their faith in him, and what exactly does it mean to do that. Those are great questions and exactly what you should be asking. I answer each of those questions in detail in Part 3 of this book.

In this chapter, I explain why Jesus took them, why you were left behind, and what this now means for you.

The Bible is God's word and contains the truth because God wrote it. God is truth. God used men to do the actual writing, but God gave them the exact words to say. Refer to Part 5 in this book to learn all about the Bible and why you can trust it. It's a wonderful love letter from God.

Every Scripture is God-breathed and profitable

for teaching, for reproof, for correction, and for instruction in righteousness, that each person who belongs to God may be complete, thoroughly equipped for every good work. (2 Timothy 3:16-17)

If we want to know why God took the people who disappeared, then we need to look for answers in the Bible. Let's start by understanding what the Bible says about the rapture.

But we don't want you to be ignorant, brothers, concerning those who have fallen asleep, so that you don't grieve like the rest, who have no hope. For if we believe that Jesus died and rose again, even so God will bring with him those who have fallen asleep in Jesus. For this we tell you by the word of the Lord, that we who are alive, who are left until the coming of the Lord, will in no way precede those who have fallen asleep. For the Lord himself will descend from heaven with a shout, with the voice of the archangel and with God's trumpet. The dead in Christ will rise first, then we who are alive, who are left, will be caught up together with them in the clouds, to meet the Lord in the air. So we will be with the Lord forever. Therefore comfort one another with these words. (1 Thessalonians 4:13-18)

Notice the phrase "caught up." In Latin it's translated *rapio*. It's where we get the English word *rapture* from. This Scripture tells us what happened to the people who vanished. Jesus came down from heaven and gathered them in the clouds with him. It tells us why Jesus took them; it's because they believed Jesus died and rose again. The people who disappeared are described as "alive" and "who are left until the coming of the Lord." They aren't the only ones Jesus took. We also learn that "the dead in Christ" were gathered too. These are people who had put their faith in Jesus, but already died. Death is also referenced in the Scripture as "fallen asleep." They died between the resurrection of Jesus and the rapture. This Scripture also gives us a glimpse of what those gathered people are doing now. It says they "will be with the Lord forever." That means they are now with Jesus, the Lord, for all eternity. If you're grieving the loss of someone who disappeared, take comfort in knowing what happened to them.

That Scripture was written by Paul the apostle in AD 51. How did he know this was going to happen and describe it in such detail? He wasn't a psychic as some of you may be thinking. Psychics get their information from Satan and demons, not God. That's why God forbids that type of activity in the Bible. Paul was one of God's prophets. He met Jesus after Jesus was resurrected, and then he believed. God spoke to Paul and showed him events that were to come. God did this for our benefit so that we could be prepared.

This Scripture was also written by Paul the apostle a few years later in AD 55. There are some clues that tell us this passage is also about the rapture. The first clue is "we will not all sleep."

> Now I say this, brothers, that flesh and blood can't inherit God's Kingdom; neither does the perishable inherit imperishable. Behold, I tell you a mystery. We will not all sleep, but we will all be changed, in a moment, in the twinkling of an eye, at the last trumpet. For the trumpet will sound and the dead will be raised incorruptible, and we will be changed. For this perishable body must become imperishable, and this mortal must put on immortality. But when this perishable body will have become imperishable, and this mortal will have put on immortality, then what is written will happen: "Death is swallowed up in victory." (1 Corinthians 15:50-54)

"Flesh and blood" is a reference to our current bodies. They're temporary and not eternal. That's why they can't live in God's kingdom, which is heaven. Paul tells us not everyone will "sleep" which means some people won't die. Instead, those people who didn't die were changed in a moment. This happened at the sound of a trumpet. That trumpet was mentioned in the prior Scripture we looked at too. That trumpet signaled the rapture. We learn some extra details about what happened to the people Jesus gathered. They got new immortal bodies that are suitable for living in heaven for eternity. In that moment, their perishable body that could die was transformed into an imperishable and immortal body.

Here's another Scripture written by Paul the apostle also in AD 51 that references the rapture.

> Now, brothers, concerning the coming of our Lord Yeshua the Messiah, and our gathering together to him, we ask you not to be quickly shaken in your mind, nor yet be troubled, either by spirit, or by word, or by letter as from us, saying that the day of Messiah had come. Let no one deceive you in any way. For it will not be, unless the departure comes first, and the man of sin is revealed, the son of destruction. (2 Thessalonians 2:1-3 HNV)

It says the "Lord Yeshua the Messiah" is coming and believers will be gathered together to him. *Messiah* means Christ or anointed by God. That's Jesus. This is about Jesus's second coming when he physically returns to earth. We learn that his second coming won't happen until "the departure" happens first. That's a reference to the rapture. Once the rapture happens, "the man of sin" is revealed. He is the Antichrist. You see, the Antichrist has a big part to play in the events to come. If the believers were still on the planet, they would prevent the Antichrist from playing his part. You're going to learn more about the Antichrist later.

This Scripture about the rapture was written by the apostle John in AD 90. John was one of Jesus's disciples and followed Jesus during his ministry. Here, John is quoting something Jesus said to his disciples before he was crucified. His disciples were believers who had put their faith in him.

> Don't let your heart be troubled. Believe in God.
> Believe also in me. In my Father's house are
> many homes. If it weren't so, I would have told
> you. I am going to prepare a place for you. If I go
> and prepare a place for you, I will come again,
> and will receive you to myself; that where I am,
> you may be there also. (John 14:1-3)

Jesus tells them to believe in God and in "me"
which is himself. Then he says there are "many
homes" in his "father's house." That's God's house. He
was leaving to go "prepare a place" for them there. We
know that God's house is in heaven. So Jesus was
leaving for heaven, and he would come get them at a
later time. This was the next thing Jesus wanted them
to be expecting: his future return to get them. The
phrase "receive you to myself" means to take to one's
self. That's literally what happened in the rapture.
Jesus took the believers to himself. He did this so that
the believers could be where he is. Jesus is currently
in heaven. In the rapture, Jesus met the believers in
the clouds and took them to himself in heaven. This
Scripture applies to anyone who puts their faith in
Jesus. The people who vanished are in God's house,
heaven, right now. If you put your faith in Jesus, you
get this promise too. Jesus has a place prepared just
for you too.

Some people have interpreted that Scripture as
being about Jesus's second coming when he physically
appears on the planet again. But that doesn't make
any sense. At Jesus's second coming, believers are
already with him in heaven and are in fact coming
with him to earth. Jesus won't be receiving or taking
anyone to himself at his second coming. No, that
Scripture is talking about the rapture.

The rapture-related Scriptures I've shared so far
have come from the New Testament books of the
Bible. So you may be thinking the rapture is a
relatively new concept and only something taught
after Jesus's death and resurrection. That's not the

case. The rapture is also mentioned in the Old Testament. Let's look at a couple Scriptures that describe the event.

Here's one written by the prophet Zephaniah in the 7th century BC. He urges people to seek God who is called "Yahweh." This is so that they can be protected or "hidden" during the day of God's anger. That's exactly what the rapture of Jesus's followers did, it protects them from God's anger.

> Seek Yahweh, all you humble of the land, who have kept his ordinances. Seek righteousness. Seek humility. It may be that you will be hidden in the day of Yahweh's anger. (Zephaniah 2:3)

This was written by King David way back in the 10th century BC. In this Scripture, he tells us that he longs to live in the house of God. He knows this is where he'll be secretly hidden during the day of trouble. That was one of the reasons for the rapture. God took the believers and has them safely hidden in heaven. They are protected from God's wrath and Satan's destruction and lies during this most difficult and perilous time.

> One thing I have asked of Yahweh, that I will seek after: that I may dwell in Yahweh's house all the days of my life, to see Yahweh's beauty, and to inquire in his temple. For in the day of trouble, he will keep me secretly in his pavilion. In the secret place of his tabernacle, he will hide me. He will lift me up on a rock. (Psalm 27:4-5)

Here's what I think is the best depiction of the rapture in the Old Testament. This Scripture was written by the prophet Isaiah in the 8th century BC. We learn similar details from this Scripture that we learned in the New Testament.

> Just as a woman with child, who draws near the time of her delivery, is in pain and cries out in her pangs, so we have been before you, Yahweh.

We have been with child. We have been in pain.
We gave birth, it seems, only to wind. We have
not worked any deliverance in the earth; neither
have the inhabitants of the world fallen. Your
dead shall live. My dead bodies shall arise.
Awake and sing, you who dwell in the dust; for
your dew is like the dew of herbs, and the earth
will cast out the departed spirits. Come, my
people, enter into your rooms, and shut your
doors behind you. Hide yourself for a little
moment, until the indignation is past. For,
behold, Yahweh comes out of his place to punish
the inhabitants of the earth for their iniquity.
(Isaiah 26:17-21)

He tells us the dead will live, the dead will arise, and
that the "earth will cast out the departed spirits." We
know this is referring to dead believers in Jesus because
they are happy and singing. There's no happiness or
singing in hell. That was the first event that happened
during the rapture; the bodies of dead believers in Jesus
were resurrected. The next phrase in Isaiah's prophecy
refers to the believers who were alive and were
raptured. It says: "come, my people, enter into your
rooms, and shut your doors." This is similar to how
Jesus described the rapture, isn't it? Jesus said he was
preparing a room for his followers and he would come
get them again. The shut door is an act of protection.
God shut the door on the ark to protect Noah and his
family during the flood. The believers were taken to
their rooms that were prepared by Jesus. The last few
sentences tell us the dead believers who were
resurrected and the believers who were raptured are
hiding themselves for a little while because God is
punishing the inhabitants of the earth for their sin.
"Iniquity" means sin. This is exactly what we learned in
the New Testament rapture Scriptures.

I hope you now see that God warned people about
the rapture and his coming judgment for thousands of
years. The people who disappeared met Jesus in the
clouds and are currently living in heaven under the
protection of God almighty.

Chapter 7 - Reasons For The Rapture

The Bible gives us insight into several reasons why the rapture took place. We're going to look at eight of those reasons in this chapter.

7.1. God Is Protecting Believers From His Wrath

God protected believers from his wrath before. During the flood, he protected Noah, his family, and the animals on the ark.

> In the six hundredth year of Noah's life, in the second month, on the seventeenth day of the month, on that day all the fountains of the great deep burst open, and the sky's windows opened. … In the same day Noah, and Shem, Ham, and Japheth—the sons of Noah—and Noah's wife and the three wives of his sons with them, entered into the ship—… then Yahweh shut him in. … The waters rose, and increased greatly on the earth; and the ship floated on the surface of the waters. (Genesis 7:11, 13, 16, 18)

When he destroyed Sodom and Gomorrah, he protected Lot and his believing family.

> When the morning came, then the angels hurried Lot, saying, "Get up! Take your wife and your two daughters who are here, lest you be consumed in the iniquity of the city." But he lingered; and the men grabbed his hand, his wife's hand, and his two daughters' hands, Yahweh being merciful to him; and they took him out, and set him outside of the city. … Then Yahweh rained on Sodom and on Gomorrah sulfur and fire from Yahweh out of the sky. (Genesis 19:15-16, 24)

The rapture is a similar type of event. During the rapture, God removed the people who had put their faith in Jesus to protect them from his wrath. The Bible tells us that believers are not meant for God's wrath. God treats believers and unbelievers differently during a time of wrath.

> Wait for his Son from heaven, whom he raised from the dead: Jesus, who delivers us from the wrath to come. (1 Thessalonians 1:10)

> For God chose to save us through our Lord Jesus Christ, not to pour out his anger on us. Christ died for us so that, whether we are dead or alive when he returns, we can live with him forever. (1 Thessalonians 5:9-10 NLT)

In those Scriptures it says Jesus delivers people from wrath. Who was it that met the raptured people in the clouds? It was Jesus. Why did they get raptured in the first place? Because they put their faith in Jesus.

So how do we know God is protecting the believers who were raptured from his wrath? In the Bible, believers are often called the "bride of Christ." The relationship believers have with Jesus is similar to the relationship married couples have. It's intimate and personal and full of love. While the raptured people are in heaven, one event they partake in is the wedding of the Lamb.

> For I married you to one husband, that I might present you as a pure virgin to Christ. (2 Corinthians 11:2)

> "Let's rejoice and be exceedingly glad, and let's give the glory to him. For the wedding of the Lamb has come, and his wife has made herself ready." It was given to her that she would array herself in bright, pure, fine linen: for the fine linen is the righteous acts of the saints. (Revelation 19:7-8)

The "Lamb" is a reference to Jesus and his act of

sacrificing himself for our sins. Before Jesus came, the Israelites sacrificed lambs to atone for their sins. Jesus is the ultimate perfect Lamb. Now you can't have a wedding without a bride. They are celebrating Jesus being married to the believers who were raptured and resurrected at the rapture, his bride.

If we look up synonyms for *husband*, we get words like *safeguard*, *steward*, *preserve*, and *hold fast*. Jesus is indeed protecting everyone he gathered to himself at the rapture.

7.2. God Is Proving He Exists

Another way God is using the rapture and the coming events is to help you see his glory and power and thus come to believe in all he's done for you. These signs and wonders, as the Bible calls them, helped many people believe in Jesus during his ministry. Miraculous signs and wonders are how we know something is from God and not from man. They point directly to God because he's the only one capable of doing them. In the last Scripture below, the references to "him" and "this man" are references to Jesus.

> People of Israel, listen! God publicly endorsed Jesus the Nazarene by doing powerful miracles, wonders, and signs through him, as you well know. (Acts 2:22 NLT)

> But of the multitude, many believed in him. They said, "When the Christ comes, he won't do more signs than those which this man has done, will he?" (John 7:31)

Even God's disciples were convinced because of Jesus's signs.

> This beginning of his signs Jesus did in Cana of Galilee, and revealed his glory; and his disciples believed in him. (John 2:11)

Here we even see that Paul the apostle was able to

do miraculous signs and wonders to display God's Spirit and bring the people to God.

> Yet I dare not boast about anything except what Christ has done through me, bringing the Gentiles to God by my message and by the way I worked among them. They were convinced by the power of miraculous signs and wonders and by the power of God's Spirit. In this way, I have fully presented the Good News of Christ from Jerusalem all the way to Illyricum. (Romans 15:18-19 NLT)

During the Old Testament times when Israel was under Egyptian captivity, God used signs and wonders to show the Egyptian Pharaoh that he was indeed God. You see, Moses demanded Pharaoh let the Israelites go free on the authority of God. Pharaoh didn't know God. Signs and wonders are how God revealed himself to Pharaoh. The Israelites didn't really know God either though. The ten plagues that God sent against Pharaoh helped the Israelites see how powerful God was. It helped them put their trust in him. Trust that he would take them out of captivity.

> Did a people ever hear the voice of God speaking out of the middle of the fire, as you have heard, and live? Or has God tried to go and take a nation for himself from among another nation, by trials, by signs, by wonders, by war, by a mighty hand, by an outstretched arm, and by great terrors, according to all that Yahweh your God did for you in Egypt before your eyes? It was shown to you so that you might know that Yahweh is God. There is no one else besides him. (Deuteronomy 4:33-35)

After God brought the Israelites out of captivity, God continued to show them signs and wonders to help strengthen their faith. A glorious example of this was God's daily provision for his people. Every day, food from heaven called manna appeared on the ground for them to gather. God revealed himself to them every single day.

> Then Yahweh said to Moses, "Behold, I will rain bread from the sky for you, and the people shall go out and gather a day's portion every day, that I may test them, whether they will walk in my law or not." ... The house of Israel called its name "Manna", and it was like coriander seed, white; and its taste was like wafers with honey. ... The children of Israel ate the manna forty years, until they came to an inhabited land. (Exodus 16:4, 31, 35)

The signs and wonders that God performed for the Israelites also helped other people groups come to believe in God. This Scripture reveals a conversation that Rahab, a prostitute in the city of Jericho, had with a couple of Israelites sent to spy on the city before an attack. She tells them that fear had fallen upon all the inhabitants of the city because they knew all that God had done for the Israelites. She spoke of God's miracle of drying up the Red Sea. They knew that God was with the Israelites. They knew that the God of Israel was the God of heaven and earth. God uses signs and wonders to reveal himself to all people.

> Before they had lain down, she came up to them on the roof. She said to the men, "I know that Yahweh has given you the land, and that the fear of you has fallen upon us, and that all the inhabitants of the land melt away before you. For we have heard how Yahweh dried up the water of the Red Sea before you, when you came out of Egypt; and what you did to the two kings of the Amorites, who were beyond the Jordan, to Sihon and to Og, whom you utterly destroyed. As soon as we had heard it, our hearts melted, and there wasn't any more spirit in any man, because of you: for Yahweh your God, he is God in heaven above, and on earth beneath." (Joshua 2:8-11)

The rapture should help you see that there is an

almighty God in heaven. A God who directs the affairs of mankind and one that we're all accountable to.

> For it is written," 'As I live,' says the Lord, 'to me every knee will bow. Every tongue will confess to God.' " So then each one of us will give account of himself to God. (Romans 14:11-12)

The miraculous things you see happening are like the end of a spectacular fireworks show. God is displaying his power for all to see so that all can come to know him. This is your last chance to be saved. Make the decision today. Don't wait for tomorrow, because tomorrow isn't guaranteed for you.

> Working together, we entreat also that you do not receive the grace of God in vain, for he says, "At an acceptable time I listened to you. In a day of salvation I helped you." Behold, now is the acceptable time. Behold, now is the day of salvation. (2 Corinthians 6:2)

I know the rapture of Jesus's believers will be known as the greatest evangelical event in history. The Bible tells us that millions of people come to know Jesus and are saved after the rapture occurs. It's because the rapture points directly to a miracle from God. Only God is capable of removing millions of people from the planet in an instant. In this Scripture below, we see a great multitude before the throne of God and before Jesus, the "Lamb." They are people saved from this time of tribulation; people who were left behind who came to put their faith in Jesus.

> After these things I looked, and behold, a great multitude, which no man could count, out of every nation and of all tribes, peoples, and languages, standing before the throne and before the Lamb, dressed in white robes, with palm branches in their hands. ... One of the elders answered, saying to me, "These who are arrayed in the white robes, who are they, and

where did they come from?" I told him, "My lord, you know." He said to me, "These are those who came out of the great suffering. They washed their robes, and made them white in the Lamb's blood." (Revelation 7:9, 13-14)

Let the worldwide sign and miracle of the rapture spark a fire and desire within you to know Jesus and believe that he died to save you. Call on Jesus's name today and be saved.

The sun will be turned into darkness, and the moon into blood, before the great and terrible day of Yahweh comes. It will happen that whoever will call on Yahweh's name shall be saved; for in Mount Zion and in Jerusalem there will be those who escape, as Yahweh has said, and among the remnant, those whom Yahweh calls. (Joel 2:31-32)

7.3. God Is Giving You A Final Warning

God wants everyone to be saved, and the rapture is signaling that this is your last chance. I think this is one of the primary reasons the rapture happened.

The Lord is not slow concerning his promise, as some count slowness; but he is patient with us, not wishing that anyone should perish, but that all should come to repentance. (2 Peter 3:9)

God wants everyone to repent of or turn from their sinful ways. He's waiting to forgive you. You just have to ask him to. Then when God forgives you, he won't remember your sins against him any longer.

Tell them, "As I live," says the Lord Yahweh, "I have no pleasure in the death of the wicked; but that the wicked turn from his way and live. Turn, turn from your evil ways! For why will you die, house of Israel? ... Again, when I say to the wicked, 'You will surely die;' if he turns from his

> sin, and does that which is lawful and right; if the wicked restore the pledge, give again that which he had taken by robbery, walk in the statutes of life, committing no iniquity; he will surely live. He will not die. None of his sins that he has committed will be remembered against him. He has done that which is lawful and right. He will surely live. Yet the children of your people say, 'The way of the Lord is not fair;' but as for them, their way is not fair." (Ezekiel 33:11, 14-17)

God loves each person he created. He created every one of us. He loves every one of us. That means he loves you. This isn't the kind of love that we understand very well. God loves with an unconditional love. He demonstrated this by sending Jesus to die for you while you were still a sinner. God doesn't place any expectations on you to be perfect before having a relationship with him. In fact, he knows that's impossible.

> For while we were yet weak, at the right time Christ died for the ungodly. For one will hardly die for a righteous man. Yet perhaps for a good person someone would even dare to die. But God commends his own love toward us, in that while we were yet sinners, Christ died for us. (Romans 5:6-8)

You're likely asking, "If God loves unconditionally then why does it seem like he's punishing me?" That's because love is just one aspect of God. God is perfect in every way. That means he's also just, holy, and righteous.

> For I will proclaim Yahweh's name. Ascribe greatness to our God! The Rock: his work is perfect, for all his ways are just. A God of faithfulness who does no wrong, just and right is he. (Deuteronomy 32:3-4)

Because God is perfect, he has to discipline and

correct those he loves. And what kind of heavenly father would he really be if he didn't correct the behavior of his children? A really terrible one. That's not God. God wants what's best for each of his children. He wants what's best for you. That means you're going to experience his corrective discipline.

> You have forgotten the exhortation which reasons with you as with children, "My son, don't take lightly the chastening of the Lord, nor faint when you are reproved by him; for whom the Lord loves, he disciplines, and chastises every son whom he receives." (Hebrews 12:5-6)

The discipline is meant to turn you to God. Remember that nothing imperfect can enter God's presence, heaven. That means you won't get to enter heaven until you're perfect. News flash: you'll never be perfect. You were imperfect the moment you were born.

> For all have sinned, and fall short of the glory of God. (Romans 3:23)

However, God sent the perfect substitute for you. He sent Jesus. If you want to live inside heaven, when God looks at you, he has to see Jesus instead, because Jesus is perfect. God can only do that if you've accepted and believe that Jesus died for you.

> For God presented Jesus as the sacrifice for sin. People are made right with God when they believe that Jesus sacrificed his life, shedding his blood. This sacrifice shows that God was being fair when he held back and did not punish those who sinned in times past, for he was looking ahead and including them in what he would do in this present time. God did this to demonstrate his righteousness, for he himself is fair and just, and he declares sinners to be right in his sight when they believe in Jesus. (Romans 3:25-26 NLT)

All of the things that are happening to you that

appear to be bad and horrible are in fact happening for your benefit. Think of a toddler who grabs at and picks up his mother's steak knife off the dinner table. The mother will immediately react and take the knife from her child. Now you know the toddler is going to scream and cry. That's what they do when people take things from them. They don't understand that the knife could have hurt them or someone else. The mother took the knife because she loves her child; she had his best interest in mind. You know the toddler didn't see it that way. This is similar to what's happening to you right now. God wants you to drop the steak knife. The knife represents all the sin in your life. Drop it so that you'll stop hurting yourself and others.

> Do you think that I like to see wicked people die? says the Sovereign LORD. Of course not! I want them to turn from their wicked ways and live. (Ezekiel 18:23 NLT)

Consider the rapture your last chance to make yourself right with God. It's a time of testing for you. Who do you love more, yourself or God? If you want to keep fulfilling your own temporary lustful desires, you'll spend eternity apart from God. Choose God, and you'll get to spend eternity in his blessings.

> Yahweh your God is testing you, to know whether you love Yahweh your God with all your heart and with all your soul. (Deuteronomy 13:3)

God used his discipline many times in the Bible to help people see their sin and turn to him. He wants you to realize you need him and that you can't save yourself. That there's an eternal consequence for being a sinner who isn't saved.

In this Scripture, the Israelites were worshiping Baal, a false god. They had completely abandoned God who delivered them out of Egyptian captivity and who fed them manna from heaven every day for 40 years. God let raiders plunder his people and take them into slavery again. But then notice what God did. He sent judges to rescue them because they cried out to God during their oppression.

> The children of Israel did that which was evil in Yahweh's sight, and served the Baals. They abandoned Yahweh, the God of their fathers, who brought them out of the land of Egypt, and followed other gods, of the gods of the peoples who were around them, and bowed themselves down to them; and they provoked Yahweh to anger. ... Yahweh's anger burned against Israel, and he delivered them into the hands of raiders who plundered them. He sold them into the hands of their enemies all around, so that they could no longer stand before their enemies. ... Yahweh raised up judges, who saved them out of the hand of those who plundered them. ... When Yahweh raised up judges for them, then Yahweh was with the judge, and saved them out of the hand of their enemies all the days of the judge; for it grieved Yahweh because of their groaning by reason of those who oppressed them and troubled them. But when the judge was dead, they turned back, and dealt more corruptly than their fathers in following other gods to serve them and to bow down to them. They didn't cease what they were doing, or give up their stubborn ways. (Judges 2:11-12, 14, 16, 18-19)

God wants you to cry out to him for help when you're distressed too. In this account, we see the prophet Jonah preaching in the city of Ninevah. Did you know that Jonah didn't want to go on this assignment? He tried to sail away from Ninevah, but guess what happened? He ended up getting swallowed by a huge fish and spit up on the shore near Nineveh. He didn't want to go because he just knew the people would repent if he told them God's judgment was coming. Jonah didn't want God to forgive them. He wanted God to punish them because of their wickedness. We are often so like Jonah. We are quick to want to see others get what's coming to them.

That's not God though. He wants everyone to repent.
That's exactly what Ninevah did when Jonah preached
to them.

> Jonah began to enter into the city a day's journey,
> and he cried out, and said, "In forty days, Nineveh
> will be overthrown!" The people of Nineveh
> believed God; and they proclaimed a fast, and put
> on sackcloth, from their greatest even to their
> least. ... God saw their works, that they turned
> from their evil way. God relented of the disaster
> which he said he would do to them, and he didn't
> do it. (Jonah 3:4-5, 10)

The city of Ninevah turned from their evil way, so
God didn't bring disaster upon them after all. That's
God's promise. If you are honestly sorry for how
you've behaved, and you don't want to act that way
anymore, when you ask God for forgiveness, he will
indeed forgive.

> I now rejoice, not that you were grieved, but that
> you were grieved to repentance. For you were
> grieved in a godly way, that you might suffer loss
> by us in nothing. For godly sorrow produces
> repentance to salvation, which brings no regret.
> But the sorrow of the world produces death. (2
> Corinthians 7:9-10)

The rapture is a key milestone event that signaled
Jesus's second coming is quickly approaching. After the
rapture, there's a period of tribulation that lasts 7 years.
In this Scripture below, everything up until "he will
make a firm covenant" has already happened. A week is
a period of 7 years. So 70 weeks is 490 years. This clock
stopped at the 69th week, when the Anointed One was
cut off. It stopped when Jesus was killed. This clock
starts again when the covenant or treaty is made with
Israel for one week, which is 7 years.

> Seventy weeks are decreed on your people and

on your holy city, to finish disobedience, and to make an end of sins, and to make reconciliation for iniquity, and to bring in everlasting righteousness, and to seal up vision and prophecy, and to anoint the most holy. Know therefore and discern that from the going out of the commandment to restore and to build Jerusalem to the Anointed One, the prince, will be seven weeks and sixty-two weeks. It will be built again, with street and moat, even in troubled times. After the sixty-two weeks the Anointed One will be cut off, and will have nothing. The people of the prince who come will destroy the city and the sanctuary. Its end will be with a flood, and war will be even to the end. Desolations are determined. He will make a firm covenant with many for one week. In the middle of the week he will cause the sacrifice and the offering to cease. On the wing of abominations will come one who makes desolate; and even to the full end, and that determined, wrath will be poured out on the desolate. (Daniel 9:24-27)

We know the person who brokers the covenant is the Antichrist because of a couple things. First, in the Scripture you just read, it said in the middle of the week he stops the sacrifices and offerings to God, then he will commit an abomination in the temple that makes it desolate because he desecrated it. A week is seven years, so the middle of the week is three and a half years. Then, in the Scriptures below, we get even more detail.

"Because you have said" is a reference to what Israel has said. Secondly, it turns out this covenant is made with death and Sheol under lies and false pretenses. "Sheol" means hell.

Because you have said, "We have made a covenant with death, and we are in agreement with Sheol. When the overflowing scourge passes through, it won't come to us; for we have made lies our refuge, and we have hidden

> ourselves under falsehood. ... Your covenant with death shall be annulled, and your agreement with Sheol shall not stand. When the overflowing scourge passes through, then you will be trampled down by it." (Isaiah 28:15, 18)

Now thirdly, we learn that this ruler who sets up the abomination exalts himself and magnifies "himself above every god." That means he declares himself god.

> Forces will stand on his part, and they will profane the sanctuary, even the fortress, and will take away the continual burnt offering. Then they will set up the abomination that makes desolate. ... The king will do according to his will. He will exalt himself, and magnify himself above every god, and will speak marvelous things against the God of gods. He will prosper until the indignation is accomplished; for that which is determined will be done. (Daniel 11:31, 36)

Who have you learned is the father of lies who said he wanted to be like God? Hell was created for him and his army. It's Satan. Satan will possess the Antichrist. Think of him as Satan in the flesh. That's who Israel brokers a deal with, and they know it.

The Bible doesn't say how much time passes between the rapture and when the tribulation starts. It could happen the same day, or it could be a year later. Based on what we learned about the flood and Sodom and Gomorrah, expect that covenant to get signed very quickly after the rapture. After God removes the righteous, he doesn't wait to send his wrath.

This should give you a sense of urgency. It's urgent that you come to believe in Jesus before you die, which could happen at any time. If you're one of the few who survive through the tribulation, you need to believe before Jesus comes back at the end of that 7 year period. Anyone who doesn't believe will be thrown into the lake of fire. Only people deemed righteous, who believe Jesus died for their sins, will be able to enter Jesus's kingdom on earth.

This is your last warning. Heed the warning like the people of Ninevah did. Believe that Jesus died for you and ask him to forgive you of your sins.

7.4. God Is Fulfilling His Promises

In some of the key rapture Scriptures in the Bible, we learn that God was fulfilling promises when he raptured the believers. One of those was Jesus's promise to return and gather his followers.

> Don't let your heart be troubled. Believe in God. Believe also in me. In my Father's house are many homes. If it weren't so, I would have told you. I am going to prepare a place for you. If I go and prepare a place for you, I will come again, and will receive you to myself; that where I am, you may be there also. (John 14:1-3)

During his ministry on earth, Jesus often spoke about heaven. He's the one speaking in the verses above. He told his disciples he was leaving, but that he'd come back to get them. While they were waiting, they should take comfort in knowing he was preparing a place for them to live with him for eternity.

Another is God's promise to resurrect the believers who had already died. There was concern among the early church believers about what happened to their loved ones who believed in Jesus but had already died prior to Jesus's second coming. They wondered if they'd get resurrected and if they'd see them again. The apostle Paul tells them to take comfort in knowing their bodies would be resurrected and made into glorious, new, eternal, immortal bodies at the rapture. In these verses, "fallen asleep" means died.

> But we don't want you to be ignorant, brothers, concerning those who have fallen asleep, so that you don't grieve like the rest, who have no hope. For if we believe that Jesus died and rose again, even so God will bring with him those who have fallen asleep in Jesus. ... The dead in Christ will

> rise first, then we who are alive, who are left, will be caught up together with them in the clouds, to meet the Lord in the air. (1 Thessalonians 4:13-14, 16-17)

This resurrection of dead believers is the first event that happened in the rapture. Then, the believers who were alive on earth were taken and met the resurrected believers and Jesus in the clouds.

God always fulfills his promises. The rapture is a great example of this. Know that you can trust God because he is faithful to do what he says he will do.

> Know therefore that Yahweh your God himself is God, the faithful God, who keeps covenant and loving kindness to a thousand generations with those who love him and keep his commandments. (Deuteronomy 7:9)

> For Jesus Christ, the Son of God, does not waver between "Yes" and "No." He is the one whom Silas, Timothy, and I preached to you, and as God's ultimate "Yes," he always does what he says. For all of God's promises have been fulfilled in Christ with a resounding "Yes!" And through Christ, our "Amen" (which means "Yes") ascends to God for his glory. (2 Corinthians 1:19-20 NLT)

If the rapture has yet to occur, you can still be included in these promises from God. If the rapture has already occurred and you're left behind, you can be included in a different promise from God. That's his promise of eternal life to those who believe. Just choose to believe in what Jesus did to save your soul; that he died for your sins, rose from the grave, and reigns in heaven.

7.5. God Is Letting Satan Reign On Earth

Another reason for the rapture is that God is letting Satan reign on earth until Jesus returns. He had to remove the believers for that to happen. God created a glorious angel, Lucifer, who was highly esteemed, wise, and ruled over other angels. One day, Lucifer got prideful and decided he could be just like God. He didn't just think it, he believed he could really do it. That's when Lucifer sinned and launched a rebellion against God. Lucifer is the "anointed cherub."

> You were the anointed cherub who covers. Then I set you up on the holy mountain of God. You have walked up and down in the middle of the stones of fire. You were perfect in your ways from the day that you were created, until unrighteousness was found in you. By the abundance of your commerce, your insides were filled with violence, and you have sinned. Therefore I have cast you as profane out of God's mountain. (Ezekiel 28:14-16)

Here we see some of that rebellion. Michael and the other good angels warred with Satan and his fallen angels. Satan, the adversary, lost. God threw him and the other rebellious angels to earth. Ever since, the earth has been under the dominion of Satan, the "devil," the "deceiver."

> There was war in the sky. Michael and his angels made war on the dragon. The dragon and his angels made war. They didn't prevail. No place was found for them any more in heaven. The great dragon was thrown down, the old serpent, he who is called the devil and Satan, the deceiver of the whole world. He was thrown down to the earth, and his angels were thrown down with him. (Revelation 12:7-9)

Even Jesus spoke about Satan falling from heaven. His disciples were astonished they could cast out demons with Jesus's name. You see, Satan is still subject to Jesus's authority. It doesn't matter where he resides, heaven or earth, God is in control.

> The seventy returned with joy, saying, "Lord, even the demons are subject to us in your name!" He said to them, "I saw Satan having fallen like lightning from heaven." (Luke 10:17-18)

Up until the rapture, Satan still had access to enter heaven and speak with God. In fact, you're going to see a bit later in this chapter that he had to ask God for permission to trouble God's people. That all changed when God removed his believers during the rapture. That's when Satan lost all of his access to heaven. In the Scripture below, Jesus told us this was going to happen. Jesus said Satan was the ruler of this world, which is earth. When the time for judging the earth comes, Satan will be cast out of heaven.

> The time for judging this world has come, when Satan, the ruler of this world, will be cast out. (John 12:31 NLT)

You've already learned that the rapture enabled God to judge the world. With the believers removed, he can send his wrath upon the wicked in hopes they will repent.

So why would God allow Satan to run amok on earth? Satan is part of God's plan. Satan is going to be dishing out all sorts of wrath after the rapture. Remember that he hates you because God loves you. And he knows he has very little time left on earth before he's cast into hell. So he's full of rage. God often uses the enemy to help people see him, his truth, and his goodness.

You know Satan wasn't God's only creation kicked out of heaven. When Adam and Eve sinned, they were kicked out of the garden of Eden, which was essentially heaven, and relegated to earth. God even stationed an angel to guard and block the way back into the garden. God also told Adam, Eve, and Satan that there would be constant hostility or hatred between them, but there was coming a day when man would bruise Satan's head. At that time, Satan would answer for his sin and crimes and spend eternity in the lake of fire. In these Scriptures below, "the man" is Adam, "the woman" is Eve, and "the serpent" is Satan.

> God said,... "Have you eaten from the tree that I commanded you not to eat from?" The man said, "The woman whom you gave to be with me, she gave me fruit from the tree, and I ate it." Yahweh God said to the woman, "What have you done?" The woman said, "The serpent deceived me, and I ate." Yahweh God said to the serpent, "Because you have done this, you are cursed above all livestock, and above every animal of the field. You shall go on your belly and you shall eat dust all the days of your life. I will put hostility between you and the woman, and between your offspring and her offspring. He will bruise your head, and you will bruise his heel." (Genesis 3:11-15)

> Yahweh God said, "Behold, the man has become like one of us, knowing good and evil. Now, lest he reach out his hand, and also take of the tree of life, and eat, and live forever—" Therefore Yahweh God sent him out from the garden of Eden, to till the ground from which he was taken. So he drove out the man; and he placed cherubim at the east of the garden of Eden, and a flaming sword which turned every way, to guard the way to the tree of life. (Genesis 3:22-24)

This is what's coming for Satan. He knows it. He knows God's word better than any of us. That's how he's able to twist God's word and deceive people. That's how he deceived Eve. I think it's even worse for us because Satan has had thousands of years to read and study all of God's word in the Bible. In this verse, the "devil" is Satan and the "beast" is the Antichrist.

> The devil who deceived them was thrown into the lake of fire and sulfur, where the beast and the false prophet are also. They will be tormented day and night forever and ever. (Revelation 20:10)

Satan has spent the last several thousand years trying to defeat God and prevent his own eternal punishment. You see, Satan still thinks he can win. After the rapture and during the tribulation period, God lets Satan have his way with mankind. However, Satan couldn't rule the earth until all the believers were removed. Anyone who's put their faith in Jesus would quickly spot the devil and his antics and hinder all of his plans. This is another reason God removed the believers, so Satan could reign.

In the Scripture below, the apostle Paul is speaking about the second coming of Jesus. He says the rebellion happens first and then the "man of sin," "son of destruction," one who exalts himself against God, one who calls himself God, and the "lawless one" is revealed. Well you should know by now that those are all descriptors of the Antichrist, Satan's man puppet, the global leader after the rapture. The Scripture even tells us this. His coming is the "working of Satan with all power and signs."

> Now, brothers, concerning the coming of our Lord Jesus Christ and our gathering together to him.... ... Let no one deceive you in any way. For it will not be, unless the rebellion comes first, and the man of sin is revealed, the son of destruction, he who opposes and exalts himself against all that is called God or that is worshiped, so that he sits as God in the temple of God, setting himself up as God. ... Now you know what is restraining him, to the end that he may be revealed in his own season. For the mystery of lawlessness already works. Only there is one who restrains now, until he is taken out of the way. Then the lawless one will be revealed, whom the Lord will kill with the breath of his mouth, and destroy by the manifestation of his coming; even he whose coming is according to the working of Satan with all power and signs and lying wonders. (2 Thessalonians 2:1, 3-4, 6-9)

Before the Antichrist could be revealed something

else had to happen first. There was "one who restrains," that was "taken out of the way." Then the lawless one, the Antichrist, is revealed. This means the restrainer was holding back the power of Satan. Only something all powerful can restrain evil. The restrainer is God's Holy Spirit, and it was living inside all the believers who were raptured.

So God also removed the believers so Satan could reign. Why would God let Satan reign? Because God loves you, that's why! It's to help you turn to God and Jesus for your salvation.

A great example of this from the Bible is Job. Job was a man of God. God said there was no one like him on earth. One day God asked Satan what he was up to on earth and if he had noticed his servant Job. Satan said he had and said Job only believed in God because God blessed him. That if God were to take away those blessings, then Job would certainly abandon God. What do think God did? In the Scriptures below, "God's sons" are angels.

> Now on the day when God's sons came to present themselves before Yahweh, Satan also came among them. Yahweh said to Satan, "Where have you come from?" Then Satan answered Yahweh, and said, "From going back and forth in the earth, and from walking up and down in it." Yahweh said to Satan, "Have you considered my servant, Job? For there is no one like him in the earth, a blameless and an upright man, one who fears God, and turns away from evil." Then Satan answered Yahweh, and said, "Does Job fear God for nothing? Haven't you made a hedge around him, and around his house, and around all that he has, on every side? You have blessed the work of his hands, and his substance is increased in the land. But stretch out your hand now, and touch all that he has, and he will renounce you to your face." (Job 1:6-11)
>
> All right, you may test him, the LORD said to Satan. "Do whatever you want with everything he possesses, but don't harm him physically." So

Satan left the LORD's presence. (Job 1:12 NLT)

God let Satan have his way with Job! I know it's a bit shocking, but he did this to test Job and his faith. To see if Job truly loved God. Job lost everything. All of his sons and daughters died, all his livestock died, and God even ended up letting Satan attack Job's health. Through all of the horrible things that happened to Job, he refused to curse God.

In all this, Job didn't sin, nor charge God with wrongdoing. (Job 1:22)

Then his wife said to him, "Do you still maintain your integrity? Renounce God, and die." But he said to her, "You speak as one of the foolish women would speak. What? Shall we receive good at the hand of God, and shall we not receive evil?" In all this Job didn't sin with his lips. (Job 2:9-10)

His faith was tested, and he passed. Afterwards, God blessed Job even more than he was blessed before. God restored his health, his wealth and livestock, and his family. God tests us so that he can reward us when we pass.

Yahweh turned the captivity of Job, when he prayed for his friends. Yahweh gave Job twice as much as he had before. ... So Yahweh blessed the latter end of Job more than his beginning. He had fourteen thousand sheep, six thousand camels, one thousand yoke of oxen, and a thousand female donkeys. He had also seven sons and three daughters. (Job 42:10, 12-13)

Something very similar is happening to you right now. God is letting Satan have his way on earth to test you and your faith. If you're left behind and you've put your faith in Jesus, this time of testing will strengthen your relationship with God, just like it did for Job. You will become unbreakable, just like Job. The Scripture below was written by Peter, one of Jesus's disciples.

He tells us the proof of our faith is more precious than gold. When you pass the testing of your faith, it brings praise, glory, honor, and most importantly the salvation of your soul.

> Wherein you greatly rejoice, though now for a little while, if need be, you have been grieved in various trials, that the proof of your faith, which is more precious than gold that perishes even though it is tested by fire, may be found to result in praise, glory, and honor at the revelation of Jesus Christ. ... Receiving the result of your faith, the salvation of your souls. Concerning this salvation, the prophets sought and searched diligently. They prophesied of the grace that would come to you, searching for who or what kind of time the Spirit of Christ, which was in them, pointed to, when he predicted the sufferings of Christ, and the glories that would follow them. To them it was revealed, that they served not themselves, but you, in these things, which now have been announced to you through those who preached the Good News to you by the Holy Spirit sent out from heaven; which things angels desire to look into. (1 Peter 1:6-7, 9-12)

If you are left behind and choose not to put your faith in Jesus, God is using Satan's reign on earth to give you exactly what you've been asking for. You don't want to believe in God or Jesus. You don't want to believe there's a heaven and hell and eternal consequences for your choices on earth. You want to live a life of sin. You want to place your faith in money and possessions. You want to be your own god. Your father isn't God, it's Satan. So God is giving you what you want; Satan as your ruler and god.

Let's see how that same decision, not choosing God, worked out for an Egyptian Pharaoh. This was during the time of Israel's captivity in Egypt. Moses demanded that Pharaoh let the people go under the authority of God. Since Pharaoh didn't know God, Moses used signs and wonders to show him and prove that God was indeed the only God.

> Moses stretched out his rod toward the heavens, and Yahweh sent thunder and hail; and lightning flashed down to the earth. Yahweh rained hail on the land of Egypt. So there was very severe hail, and lightning mixed with the hail, such as had not been in all the land of Egypt since it became a nation. The hail struck throughout all the land of Egypt all that was in the field, both man and animal; and the hail struck every herb of the field, and broke every tree of the field. ... Pharaoh sent and called for Moses and Aaron, and said to them, "I have sinned this time. Yahweh is righteous, and I and my people are wicked. Pray to Yahweh; for there has been enough of mighty thunderings and hail. I will let you go, and you shall stay no longer." Moses said to him, "As soon as I have gone out of the city, I will spread out my hands to Yahweh. The thunders shall cease, and there will not be any more hail; that you may know that the earth is Yahweh's." ... When Pharaoh saw that the rain and the hail and the thunders had ceased, he sinned yet more, and hardened his heart, he and his servants. The heart of Pharaoh was hardened, and he didn't let the children of Israel go, just as Yahweh had spoken through Moses. (Exodus 9:23-25, 27-29, 34-35)

During the plague of severe hail, Pharaoh realized he had sinned and was wicked and that God was righteous. However, as soon as God's wrath of the plague went away, he sinned even more and hardened his heart. He knew the truth, but he refused to believe it. He was stubborn, like a stone. Jesus spoke about people like this, people who don't want to believe. Look at what he said.

> Therefore Jesus said to them, "If God were your father, you would love me, for I came out and have come from God. For I haven't come of myself, but

he sent me. Why don't you understand my speech? Because you can't hear my word. You are of your father, the devil, and you want to do the desires of your father. He was a murderer from the beginning, and doesn't stand in the truth, because there is no truth in him. When he speaks a lie, he speaks on his own; for he is a liar, and the father of lies. But because I tell the truth, you don't believe me." (John 8:42-45)

If you don't want to have anything to do with God, he isn't going to force you to. You know God is so good to every single one of us because he gives us exactly what we ask for. If you are left behind, it's because you didn't choose to believe in Jesus. Instead, you were living a life of sin, following in the footsteps of your authority, Satan. During this time of tribulation, Satan is physically ruling on the earth through the Antichrist. God has given you exactly what you wanted. The Bible tells us these people continue to shake their fist at God, just like Pharaoh did, throughout all the plagues God brings upon the earth during the tribulation.

> The rest of mankind, who were not killed with these plagues, didn't repent of the works of their hands, that they wouldn't worship demons, and the idols of gold, and of silver, and of brass, and of stone, and of wood; which can't see, hear, or walk. They didn't repent of their murders, their sorceries, their sexual immorality, or their thefts. (Revelation 9:20-21)

> They gnawed their tongues because of the pain, and they blasphemed the God of heaven because of their pains and their sores. They still didn't repent of their works. (Revelation 16:10-11)

However, you can make a different choice today. You don't have to be like Pharaoh. You don't have to be like those people who refuse to repent of their sin. You don't have to let this time of testing harden your heart. Let this time of Satan's reign show you how truly evil he is and how good God is. Observe the mighty power of God during this time and choose to believe. Have faith like Job did, and you will overcome and be blessed.

7.6. God Is Punishing Wickedness

Since God is just, he has to punish wickedness. Think of how angry you get when someone wrongs you. You want justice for the wrong they committed against you. God wants justice for the wrong we sinful people commit against him too.

> God is an honest judge. He is angry with the wicked every day. (Psalm 7:11 NLT)

God is able to judge and punish because he's the one true judge of righteousness. It's because he is perfect and holy and just. He created everything and made the rules and the law for us to live by.

> God alone, who gave the law, is the Judge. He alone has the power to save or to destroy. (James 4:12 NLT)

> He is the Rock; his deeds are perfect. Everything he does is just and fair. He is a faithful God who does no wrong; how just and upright he is! (Deuteronomy 32:4 NLT)

> They sang the song of Moses, the servant of God, and the song of the Lamb, saying, "Great and marvelous are your works, Lord God, the Almighty! Righteous and true are your ways, you King of the nations." (Revelation 15:3)

Our choices have a consequence because God is the judge that we're accountable to. See Romans 14:11-12 in Chapter 7.2.

Since God is righteous and just, he can't ignore wickedness. He must do something about it.

Wickedness continually grows and eventually becomes a large volume of people who've turned away from God. People ignore God's word. People refuse to believe God exists and that God demands and deserves our worship. This requires God's intervention because God is the ultimate judge. You don't like it when people commit a crime against you and then get away with it and go unpunished. How do you think God feels? God sees everything. God knows everything. God does not let wickedness go unpunished.

In this Scripture, God spoke to King Solomon and warned him what would happen if the people turned away from God and worshiped false gods. God would uproot them from the land he gave them and make them an object of ridicule.

> But if you turn away and forsake the decrees and commands I have given you and go off to serve other gods and worship them, then I will uproot Israel from my land, which I have given them, and will reject this temple I have consecrated for my Name. I will make it a byword and an object of ridicule among all peoples. This temple will become a heap of rubble. All who pass by will be appalled and say, "Why has the LORD done such a thing to this land and to this temple?" People will answer, "Because they have forsaken the LORD, the God of their ancestors, who brought them out of Egypt, and have embraced other gods, worshiping and serving them—that is why he brought all this disaster on them." (2 Chronicles 7:19-22 NIV)

This is exactly what's happening now for those of you left behind. You've turned away from God. You're worshiping idols, yourself, demons, plants, animals, you name it. The apostle Paul doesn't hold anything back in telling us why the wrath of God is upon mankind during the tribulation period. I counted thirty-five accusations against evil mankind in these verses.

> For the wrath of God is revealed from heaven against all ungodliness and unrighteousness of men who suppress the truth in unrighteousness, because that which is known of God is revealed in them, for God revealed it to them. For the invisible things of him since the creation of the world are clearly seen, being perceived through the things that are made, even his everlasting power and divinity, that they may be without excuse. Because knowing God, they didn't glorify him as God, and didn't give thanks, but became vain in their reasoning, and their senseless heart was darkened. ... Who exchanged the truth of God for a lie, and worshiped and served the creature rather than the Creator, who is blessed forever. ... Being filled with all unrighteousness, sexual immorality, wickedness, covetousness, malice; full of envy, murder, strife, deceit, evil habits, secret slanderers, backbiters, hateful to God, insolent, arrogant, boastful, inventors of evil things, disobedient to parents, without understanding, covenant breakers, without natural affection, unforgiving, unmerciful; who, knowing the ordinance of God, that those who practice such things are worthy of death, not only do the same, but also approve of those who practice them. (Romans 1:18-21, 25, 29-32)

God sees and knows everything. He hears the cries of people who are oppressed and persecuted. When Cain murdered his brother Abel, God said the voice of Abel's blood cried out to him from the ground.

> Cain said to Abel, his brother, "Let's go into the field." While they were in the field, Cain rose up against Abel, his brother, and killed him. Yahweh said to Cain, "Where is Abel, your brother?" He said, "I don't know. Am I my brother's keeper?" Yahweh said, "What have you done? The voice of your brother's blood cries to me from the ground." (Genesis 4:8-10)

As judge, God doesn't let wickedness go unpunished. Once the cries are loud enough, he responds. When the Egyptians enslaved the Israelites, they cried to God for deliverance. God heard them and rescued them. God had to send plagues upon Egypt and against the Pharaoh before he would let the people go. God punished Pharaoh's wickedness against the Israelites.

> The Egyptians mistreated us, afflicted us, and imposed hard labor on us. Then we cried to Yahweh, the God of our fathers. Yahweh heard our voice, and saw our affliction, our toil, and our oppression. Yahweh brought us out of Egypt with a mighty hand, with an outstretched arm, with great terror, with signs, and with wonders. (Deuteronomy 26:6-8)

God ordained this time of tribulation because of the wickedness on the earth. He heard the cries of the people and of the earth itself, and he has responded. Here, we see people who died during the tribulation period because they believed in Jesus. They are asking God when he will avenge their deaths. In these verses, the "Lamb" refers to Jesus.

> When he opened the fifth seal, I saw underneath the altar the souls of those who had been killed for the Word of God, and for the testimony of the Lamb which they had. They cried with a loud voice, saying, "How long, Master, the holy and true, until you judge and avenge our blood on those who dwell on the earth?" (Revelation 6:9-10)

The Bible says vengeance is God's.

> "Vengeance belongs to me. I will repay," says the Lord. Again, "The Lord will judge his people." It is a fearful thing to fall into the hands of the living God. (Hebrews 10:30-31)

In the Scripture here, Jesus is the one who

answered when questioned about the end of the age. Notice that he says they are days of vengeance. God's divine vengeance.

> They asked him, "Teacher, so when will these things be? What is the sign that these things are about to happen?" ... "For these are days of vengeance, that all things which are written may be fulfilled." (Luke 21:7, 22)

This is one of the reasons the rapture happened, so God could punish the wicked and avenge himself and his believers. How are you going to respond during this difficult time? Go back to those verses above from Romans and do what those who refuse to repent won't do. Recognize God's authority, glorify God, give thanks to God, accept God's truth, worship and serve only God, and be filled with righteousness by placing your faith in Jesus.

7.7. God Is Preparing For Jesus's Millennial Kingdom

God is also using the rapture and the events taking place in the tribulation period to prepare for the second coming of Jesus. Jesus is physically coming back to earth at the end of the seven year tribulation period. Jesus spoke about this during his ministry on earth. He says immediately after the suffering, that's the tribulation period, his sign would appear in the sky. Then all those who believe in him will be gathered. "As he sat" refers to Jesus, and he's the one who answers the disciples question about the end of the age.

> As he sat on the Mount of Olives, the disciples came to him privately, saying, "Tell us, when will these things be? What is the sign of your coming, and of the end of the age?" ... "But immediately after the suffering of those days...the sign of the Son of Man will appear in the sky. Then all the tribes of the earth will mourn, and they will see

the Son of Man coming on the clouds of the sky with power and great glory. He will send out his angels with a great sound of a trumpet, and they will gather together his chosen ones from the four winds, from one end of the sky to the other." (Matthew 24:3, 29-31)

Jesus returns to set up his kingdom on earth. He will reign on earth for 1,000 years or a millennium. Prior to this event, God must separate those who believe in Jesus from those who don't. You see, only those who believe in Jesus will get to join Jesus's kingdom. It doesn't matter when in time the person lived. As long as they had placed their faith in Jesus, they're in. This means all the believers who were raptured, believers who die after the rapture, and believers still alive at the time of Jesus's second coming. It also includes all who were counted as righteous before Jesus died for our sins, the Old Testament believers.

This Scripture is describing what's going on at Jesus's second coming. The armies "followed him" which is Jesus. Out of Jesus's mouth is a sharp sword, that's his word. Jesus will rule. We learn that all the believers get to live and some even reign with Jesus during his 1,000 year kingdom. If you are left behind, this could be your future if you choose to believe in Jesus.

The armies which are in heaven followed him on white horses, clothed in white, pure, fine linen. Out of his mouth proceeds a sharp, double-edged sword, that with it he should strike the nations. He will rule them with an iron rod. ... I saw thrones, and they sat on them, and judgment was given to them. I saw the souls of those who had been beheaded for the testimony of Jesus, and for the word of God, and such as didn't worship the beast nor his image, and didn't receive the mark on their forehead and on their hand. They lived and reigned with Christ for a thousand years. The rest of the dead didn't live until the thousand years were finished. This is the first resurrection. Blessed and holy is he who has part in the first resurrection. Over these, the second death has no power, but they will be priests of God and of Christ, and will reign with him one thousand years. (Revelation 19:14-15, 20:4-6)

If you are left behind and you don't put your faith in Jesus, then you don't want to live with Jesus in eternity. God lets you make that choice and then he honors it. If you are still alive at the time of Jesus's second coming and you still don't believe in him, and you still haven't put your salvation in the nail pierced hands of Jesus, then you will get thrown into the lake of fire. In this Scripture, the "Son of Man" and the "King" are references to Jesus. It's a Scripture that further details Jesus's second coming. The "sheep" are those who believe in Jesus, the "goats" are those who don't.

But when the Son of Man comes in his glory, and all the holy angels with him, then he will sit on the throne of his glory. Before him all the nations will be gathered, and he will separate them one from another, as a shepherd separates the sheep from the goats. He will set the sheep on his right hand, but the goats on the left. Then the King will tell those on his right hand, "Come, blessed of my Father, inherit the Kingdom prepared for you from the foundation of the world." ... Then he will say also to those on the left hand, "Depart from me, you cursed, into the eternal fire which is prepared for the devil and his angels." (Matthew 25:31-34, 41)

Eternal fire, such an unfortunate end after enduring such hardship after the rapture. You can still be included in Jesus's millennial kingdom on earth. Choose to put your faith in Jesus like those who were raptured did.

7.8. God Is Preparing Believers For Millennial

Reign With Jesus

Another reason the rapture occurred is because God needed to gather all his believers so that he could prepare them to reign with Jesus. You already know those gathered believers are in heaven with God and Jesus. Now they are being prepared to rule with Jesus during his 1,000-year reign on the earth. Yes, you read that right. The people who were gathered will be rulers on the earth with Jesus.

> Blessed and holy is he who has part in the first resurrection. Over these, the second death has no power, but they will be priests of God and of Christ, and will reign with him one thousand years. (Revelation 20:6)

Recall that the rapture gathered two groups of people: believers alive at the time of the rapture and believers who had already died. See 1 Thessalonians 4:16-17 in Chapter 7.4.

When the gathered believers were taken to heaven, they became holy. They were taken because they were considered righteous, not because they always behaved righteously. Jesus is the only one who's perfect. When a person puts their faith in Jesus, they are immediately stamped as righteous. Over time, God's Holy Spirit will then help that person become more and more pure. It's a process called sanctification. However, it's not until getting to heaven that believers attain that perfection.

> Work at living in peace with everyone, and work at living a holy life, for those who are not holy will not see the Lord. (Hebrews 12:14 NLT)

> The LORD will perfect [that which] concerns me. (Psalm 138:8 NKJV)

> May the God of peace himself sanctify you completely. May your whole spirit, soul, and body be preserved blameless at the coming of

> our Lord Jesus Christ. He who calls you is
> faithful, who will also do it. (1 Thessalonians
> 5:23-24)

Now that those believers have attained that perfect
behavior and no longer sin, they're prepared to reign
justly with Jesus. This is one of the reasons why Jesus
couldn't set up his kingdom the first time he came to
earth. He had to die for our sins first. Then he needed
to wait patiently in heaven for people to put their faith
in him. Remember that God wants everyone to be
saved. Then at the right time, he gathered all those
believers to himself, gave them glorified immortal
bodies, and removed their ability to sin. The millennial
kingdom will be ruled by Jesus and completely
righteous people. How different and wonderful it will
be from anything any of us have ever known.

The Bible also tells us that the people who were
raptured are also in heaven receiving crowns for their
service on earth. Only a few types of crowns are
mentioned, but there could be any number of them.
Let's see what sorts of crowns the raptured people are
getting.

There's a crown for believers who exhibited self-
control called the incorruptible crown.

> Every man who strives in the games exercises self-
> control in all things. Now they do it to receive a
> corruptible crown, but we an incorruptible. (1
> Corinthians 9:25)

There's a crown of rejoicing for believers who won
souls for Jesus.

> For what is our hope, or joy, or crown of
> rejoicing? Isn't it even you, before our Lord
> Jesus at his coming? (1 Thessalonians 2:19)

For believers who lead other believers, like elders and
pastors, and did a good job, there's the crown of glory.

> Therefore I exhort the elders among you, as a fellow elder, and a witness of the sufferings of Christ, and who will also share in the glory that will be revealed: Shepherd the flock of God which is among you, exercising the oversight, not under compulsion, but voluntarily, not for dishonest gain, but willingly; not as lording it over those entrusted to you, but making yourselves examples to the flock. When the chief Shepherd is revealed, you will receive the crown of glory that doesn't fade away. (1 Peter 5:1-4)

Some of the believers who were raptured were looking forward to that day. They get the crown of righteousness.

> From now on, the crown of righteousness is stored up for me, which the Lord, the righteous judge, will give to me on that day; and not to me only, but also to all those who have loved his appearing. (2 Timothy 4:8)

If you are left behind and come to put your salvation in the hands of Jesus, you too could get a crown and rule with Jesus during the millennial period. This is certainly a special crown and one that's very difficult to achieve. You see, you'll have to be martyred for your unwavering faith in Jesus during the tribulation period. You cannot worship the Antichrist, the "beast," and you cannot receive his mark. If you are faithful to Jesus up until you die, you'll get the crown of life. And you too will get to reign with Jesus during his millennial kingdom on earth. See also Revelation 7:9, 13-14 in Chapter 7.2.

> I saw thrones, and they sat on them, and judgment was given to them. I saw the souls of those who had been beheaded for the testimony of Jesus, and for the word of God, and such as didn't worship the beast nor his image, and didn't receive the mark on their forehead and on

their hand. They lived and reigned with Christ for a thousand years. (Revelation 20:4)

Don't be afraid of the things which you are about to suffer. Behold, the devil is about to throw some of you into prison, that you may be tested; and you will have oppression for ten days. Be faithful to death, and I will give you the crown of life (Revelation 2:10)

You'll join honorable company. Many of Jesus's disciples died for their faith. In the verses below, you can see that James was killed by a "sword." Jesus told Peter he would die by crucifixion which is described by "stretch out your hands." Stephen was "stoned" to death. They were all disciples of Jesus who died for their faith.

Now about that time, King Herod stretched out his hands to oppress some of the assembly. He killed James, the brother of John, with the sword. (Acts 12:1-2)

Most certainly I tell you, when you were young, you dressed yourself and walked where you wanted to. But when you are old, you will stretch out your hands, and another will dress you and carry you where you don't want to go. (John 21:18)

"You stiff-necked and uncircumcised in heart and ears, you always resist the Holy Spirit! As your fathers did, so you do. Which of the prophets didn't your fathers persecute? They killed those who foretold the coming of the Righteous One, of whom you have now become betrayers and murderers. You received the law as it was ordained by angels, and didn't keep it!" Now when they heard these things, they were cut to the heart, and they gnashed at him with their teeth. ... They stoned Stephen. (Acts 7:51-54, 59)

Most important of all, Jesus died for his unwavering

faith in God's ability to save you through his death. Jesus was martyred to save your soul. It wasn't easy for him. He knew he was going to be crucified; it's what he came to earth for. He knew what he was going to have to endure. Jesus is the one speaking in these verses.

> Now my soul is troubled. What shall I say? "Father, save me from this time?" But I came to this time for this cause. (John 12:27)

> Then Jesus came with them to a place called Gethsemane....... Then he said to them, "My soul is exceedingly sorrowful, even to death. Stay here and watch with me." He went forward a little, fell on his face, and prayed, saying, "My Father, if it is possible, let this cup pass away from me; nevertheless, not what I desire, but what you desire." (Matthew 26:36, 38-39)

Jesus had a completely human body. He felt pain just like we do.

> For it is better, if it is God's will, that you suffer for doing well than for doing evil. Because Christ also suffered for sins once, the righteous for the unrighteous, that he might bring you to God, being put to death in the flesh, but made alive in the Spirit. (1 Peter 3:17-18)

Jesus overcame, and his martyred disciples overcame because they had the Holy Spirit living inside of them. If you put your faith in Jesus, you can overcome as well.

Now that you understand God's purposes for the rapture, I hope you come to know him and trust him as a result. Choose to believe that Jesus loves you and died for you. Accept his gift of salvation.

Chapter 8 - Rapture Questions And Answers

I know you must still have lots of questions about what's happened and why. Here are answers to some questions I thought you would ask me if you could.

8.1. Why Was I Left Behind?

8.1.1. I'm A Good Person?

No, you're not a good person. The people who were raptured weren't taken because they were good people either. Remember that the Bible tells us that no one is a good person.

> There is no one who does good, no, not so much as one. (Romans 3:12)

> For all have sinned, and fall short of the glory of God. (Romans 3:23)

You have to realize that God, not humans, is the judge of what is good. If humans were determining this, we'd each have a different standard. So then where would we be? Whose standard would get used? That just doesn't work. We're not little gods. Instead, God is the standard. God says you have to be perfect to be in his presence and live in heaven. We're not perfect and God knows that. That's why he sent Jesus, his son. The punishment for sin is death. God placed everyone's sins upon Jesus and crucified him for our sins. Jesus died to save everyone. God resurrected Jesus to show that death was conquered. God did this to show you how much he loves you. You just have to be reconciled to God by choosing to believe.

> Therefore if anyone is in Christ, he is a new creation. The old things have passed away. Behold, all things have become new. But all

things are of God, who reconciled us to himself through Jesus Christ, and gave to us the ministry of reconciliation; namely, that God was in Christ reconciling the world to himself, not reckoning to them their trespasses, and having committed to us the word of reconciliation. We are therefore ambassadors on behalf of Christ, as though God were entreating by us: we beg you on behalf of Christ, be reconciled to God. For him who knew no sin he made to be sin on our behalf; so that in him we might become the righteousness of God. (2 Corinthians 5:17-21)

God didn't rapture people because of anything they had done; it was about what they believed God did for them.

8.1.2. I Believe In God?

Believing in God is only part of what's required. You see, even the demons believe that.

You say you have faith, for you believe that there is one God. Good for you! Even the demons believe this, and they tremble in terror. (James 2:19 NLT)

You must also recognize that you are a sinner and thus unable to live in heaven with God until you solve your sin problem.

But your iniquities have separated you and your God, and your sins have hidden his face from you. (Isaiah 59:2)

You must believe that God sent his son Jesus to die for your sins. That's the only way to heaven; through Jesus.

"Don't let your heart be troubled. Believe in God. Believe also in me." ... Jesus said to him, "I am the way, the truth, and the life. No one comes to the Father, except through me." (John 14:1, 6)

8.1.3. I Grew Up In A Christian Home?

Being a believer requires you to make a personal decision about Jesus. Another person can't make that decision for you. The best another person can do to help you become a believer is to pray for you. By praying for you, they're asking God to help you come to know him and what Jesus did for you. You are accountable to God for your own sin. No one else is.

> Yahweh commanded, saying, "The fathers shall not be put to death for the children, nor the children be put to death for the fathers; but every man shall die for his own sin." (2 Kings 14:6)

> For it is written," 'As I live,' says the Lord, 'to me every knee will bow. Every tongue will confess to God.' " So then each one of us will give account of himself to God. (Romans 14:11-12)

In this Scripture, we learn our heart has to be right with God, and that change is produced from God's Spirit. That's the Holy Spirit that believers receive when they put their faith in Jesus.

> For you are not a true Jew just because you were born of Jewish parents or because you have gone through the ceremony of circumcision. No, a true Jew is one whose heart is right with God. And true circumcision is not merely obeying the letter of the law; rather, it is a change of heart produced by God's Spirit. And a person with a changed heart seeks praise from God, not from people. (Romans 2:28-29 NLT)

Jesus approaches each person and knocks on the door of their heart. Each person must choose to open the door and invite him in.

> Behold, I stand at the door and knock. If anyone

hears my voice and opens the door, then I will come in to him, and will dine with him, and he with me. He who overcomes, I will give to him to sit down with me on my throne, as I also overcame, and sat down with my Father on his throne. (Revelation 3:20-21)

Let's consider Judas. He was one of Jesus's original twelve disciples. He lived and traveled with Jesus, heard all of his teachings, and saw all the miracles. He had a front row seat. Judas wasn't saved because he didn't believe. He was surrounded by Jesus, but never placed his faith in him. He didn't have that personal relationship with Jesus that's necessary for salvation. Because Judas didn't believe, Satan was able to possess him and get him to betray Jesus. In the second Scripture below, Jesus is the one reclining at the table with his disciples.

Satan entered into Judas, who was also called Iscariot, who was counted with the twelve. He went away, and talked with the chief priests and captains about how he might deliver him to them. (Luke 22:3-4)

Now when evening had come, he was reclining at the table with the twelve disciples. As they were eating, he said, "Most certainly I tell you that one of you will betray me. ... The Son of Man goes even as it is written of him, but woe to that man through whom the Son of Man is betrayed! It would be better for that man if he had not been born." Judas, who betrayed him, answered, "It isn't me, is it, Rabbi?" He said to him, "You said it." (Matthew 26:20-21, 24-25)

Jesus told his disciples it was better for his betrayer if he had never been born. That's because although Judas "grew up" with Jesus, he didn't believe in Jesus. So his eternal residence is the lake of fire.

8.1.4. I Was Baptized?

Being baptized will not save you. That would mean you did something to get to heaven. You can't earn your way into heaven. It's by faith that you get in, not by your works. It's about what God did for you. As the second Scripture here says, we are justified by faith.

> For by grace you have been saved through faith, and that not of yourselves; it is the gift of God, not of works, that no one would boast. (Ephesians 2:8-9)

> What then will we say that Abraham, our forefather, has found according to the flesh? For if Abraham was justified by works, he has something to boast about, but not toward God. For what does the Scripture say? "Abraham believed God, and it was accounted to him for righteousness."... Now it was not written that it was accounted to him for his sake alone, but for our sake also, to whom it will be accounted, who believe in him who raised Jesus, our Lord, from the dead. ... Being therefore justified by faith, we have peace with God through our Lord Jesus Christ. (Romans 4:1-3, 23-24, 5:1)

If you are counting on something other than faith to save you, like your baptism or your circumcision, then you are not saved.

> Listen! I, Paul, tell you this: If you are counting on circumcision to make you right with God, then Christ will be of no benefit to you. ... For if you are trying to make yourselves right with God by keeping the law, you have been cut off from Christ! You have fallen away from God's grace. But we who live by the Spirit eagerly wait to receive by faith the righteousness God has promised to us. For when we place our faith in Christ Jesus, there is no benefit in being circumcised or being uncircumcised. What is

important is faith expressing itself in love. (Galatians 5:2, 4-6 NLT)

The Bible does say you should get baptized, but not in order to save your soul. Believers are meant to get baptized to demonstrate their faith and show the decision they made to believe in Jesus. Much like you have a wedding ceremony to celebrate and demonstrate the relationship you have with your spouse, baptism celebrates and shows the relationship you have with Jesus. Peter, one of Jesus's disciples, tells us baptism is a response to God from a clean conscience. You only get a clean conscience once you place your faith in Jesus.

> And that water is a picture of baptism, which now saves you, not by removing dirt from your body, but as a response to God from a clean conscience. It is effective because of the resurrection of Jesus Christ. (1 Peter 3:21 NLT)

A good example from the Bible is the thief who was on the cross next to Jesus. Jesus told him he'd be in paradise with him that day, yet he never got baptized, and he died after Jesus died. He was saved because of his faith. This Scripture is an account of Jesus's crucifixion with two criminals.

> There were also others, two criminals, led with him to be put to death. When they came to the place that is called "The Skull", they crucified him there with the criminals, one on the right and the other on the left. ... One of the criminals who was hanged insulted him, saying, "If you are the Christ, save yourself and us!" But the other answered, and rebuking him said, "Don't you even fear God, seeing you are under the same condemnation? And we indeed justly, for we receive the due reward for our deeds, but this man has done nothing wrong." He said to Jesus, "Lord, remember me when you come into your Kingdom." Jesus said to him, "Assuredly I tell you, today you will be with me in Paradise."

(Luke 23:32-33, 39-43)

Another point from the Bible is that Jesus didn't baptize anyone. If that was something that was required to enter heaven, don't you think Jesus would have gone everywhere baptizing everyone? The apostle Paul explains that to us because he didn't go around baptizing people either. It's because they were both sent to preach the Good News because that's what saves people.

> For Christ sent me not to baptize, but to preach the Good News—not in wisdom of words, so that the cross of Christ wouldn't be made void. (1 Corinthians 1:17)

Getting into heaven, being considered a believer, living in eternity with God, and being saved is about one thing only: your belief that Jesus died for your sins.

8.1.5. I Went To Church?

Being saved isn't about what you've done or, as the Bible calls it, your works. You can't earn your way into heaven. See Ephesians 2:8-9 in Chapter 8.1.4.

The way into heaven is believing that Jesus is the way. See John 14:6 in Chapter 8.1.2.

If you attended church and learned about God, Jesus, and perhaps even the rapture, that doesn't mean you've placed your faith in Jesus. To be saved, you need to have a relationship with Jesus. This Scripture is speaking of Jesus when it says "in him."

> In him you also, having heard the word of the truth, the Good News of your salvation—in whom, having also believed, you were sealed with the promised Holy Spirit. (Ephesians 1:13)

Once you believe in Jesus, you are sealed with his Holy Spirit, and you and Jesus become one. Just as this Scripture describes. In this Scripture, Jesus is the one praying.

[I pray] that they may all be one; even as you, Father, are in me, and I in you, that they also may be one in us; that the world may believe that you sent me. The glory which you have given me, I have given to them; that they may be one, even as we are one; I in them, and you in me, that they may be perfected into one; that the world may know that you sent me and loved them, even as you loved me. (John 17:21-23)

The act of attending church will not save you. It's what you hear and read at church and come to believe about Jesus that will save you. You must place your faith in Jesus to be saved.

8.1.6. I've Read The Bible?

Being knowledgeable about the Bible, God, Jesus, etc. won't save you. You have to be born again. There's a great example of this in the Bible. His name was Nicodemus. He was a Pharisee, a man highly educated and studied in the Jewish scriptures. He was likely a teacher of the scriptures himself. He asked Jesus what it took to be saved. Here's what Jesus said to him.

Jesus answered him, "Most certainly, I tell you, unless one is born anew, he can't see God's Kingdom." Nicodemus said to him, "How can a man be born when he is old? Can he enter a second time into his mother's womb, and be born?" Jesus answered, "Most certainly I tell you, unless one is born of water and spirit, he can't enter into God's Kingdom. That which is born of the flesh is flesh. That which is born of the Spirit is spirit." (John 3:3-6)

Jesus didn't tell him to go read the Scriptures and memorize everything. No, Jesus told him he needed to be born again of the Spirit. That's a reference to God's Holy Spirit. And you get the Holy Spirit once you've placed your faith in Jesus.

8.1.7. I Volunteered At Church?

Volunteering at church or doing other good works in the name of God or Jesus doesn't make you a believer, and it won't save your soul. In this Scripture, Jesus is the one speaking, and he addresses this exact problem: people who've done good works in Jesus's name but aren't able to enter heaven. Jesus said he never knew them. Of course he knew who they were, but he means that he didn't have a relationship with them.

> Not everyone who says to me, "Lord, Lord," will enter into the Kingdom of Heaven, but he who does the will of my Father who is in heaven. Many will tell me in that day, "Lord, Lord, didn't we prophesy in your name, in your name cast out demons, and in your name do many mighty works?" Then I will tell them, "I never knew you. Depart from me, you who work iniquity." (Matthew 7:21-23)

Remember that being saved is about God's grace and his love for you. It's not about your accomplishments or how hard you work for him. It comes down to believing and having a relationship with Jesus. That's the only work God requires of you; that you believe in Jesus.

> Jesus told them, "This is the only work God wants from you: Believe in the one he has sent." (John 6:29 NLT)

Then you will be accounted as righteous because you believe.

> Now to him who works, the reward is not counted as grace, but as something owed. But to him who doesn't work, but believes in him who justifies the ungodly, his faith is accounted for righteousness. (Romans 4:4-5)

8.1.8. I Gave Money To God's Work?

Giving money to a church or to other organizations that do God's work will not get you into heaven. You can't buy or earn your way into God's presence. In these two Scriptures, Jesus is the one speaking to the Pharisees. They were giving money as well, but they disregarded what was most important: faith.

> Woe to you, scribes and Pharisees, hypocrites! For you tithe mint, dill, and cumin, and have left undone the weightier matters of the law: justice, mercy, and faith. But you ought to have done these, and not to have left the other undone (Matthew 23:23)

> What sorrow awaits you Pharisees! For you are careful to tithe even the tiniest income from your herb gardens, but you ignore justice and the love of God. You should tithe, yes, but do not neglect the more important things. (Luke 11:42 NLT)

Just because you're giving to God's work doesn't mean you know Jesus and believe he died for your sins. See Matthew 7:21-23 in Chapter 8.1.7. Jesus is the one speaking in this Scripture too, and he says many people who did good works in his name won't get into heaven. It's because he never knew them. Jesus's Holy Spirit never lived inside of them because they never placed their faith in Jesus.

You need to make a choice between worshiping God and worshiping money. I know especially today that it seems like money can solve all of your problems. I agree that it can certainly solve a lot of your earthly problems. The problem with that approach is that your life in your current body on earth is just a vapor compared to eternity. Having money can make it hard for you to realize you need God in your life. A young rich man approached Jesus one day and asked what he needed to do to gain eternal life. Here's what Jesus told him.

> Behold, one came to him and said, "Good teacher, what good thing shall I do, that I may have eternal life?" ... Jesus said to him, "If you want to be perfect, go, sell what you have, and give to the poor, and you will have treasure in heaven; and come, follow me." But when the young man heard this, he went away sad, for he was one who had great possessions. Jesus said to his disciples, "Most certainly I say to you, a rich man will enter into the Kingdom of Heaven with difficulty." (Matthew 19:16, 21-23)

Jesus told him to sell all of his stuff, give it to the poor, and then come and follow him. Jesus wanted to see who or what he loved most. Since the rich man went away sad, it seems he loved his stuff more than Jesus. This is because it's impossible to worship both God and money. It's one or the other. In this Scripture, "mammon" means money or treasure.

> No one can serve two masters, for either he will hate the one and love the other, or else he will be devoted to one and despise the other. You can't serve both God and Mammon. (Matthew 6:24)

Surrender to God, and he'll provide for you. Remember that the only thing God requires of you to be saved is that you believe in Jesus. See Ephesians 2:8-9 in Chapter 8.1.4 and John 6:29 in Chapter 8.1.7. When you decide to believe in Jesus, then the money you're donating for God's work won't be in vain. You'll be giving from a clean heart that's been washed by the Holy Spirit. You'll be storing up treasure in heaven.

> Don't lay up treasures for yourselves on the earth, where moth and rust consume, and where thieves break through and steal; but lay up for yourselves treasures in heaven, where neither moth nor rust consume, and where thieves don't break through and steal; for where your treasure is, there your heart will be also. (Matthew 6:19-21)

8.2. Why Were These People Raptured?

8.2.1. People Who Didn't Look Like Christians?

Christians, people who've put their saving faith in Jesus's death and resurrection, don't have to look a particular way. They'll come from all walks of life, all cultures, all nations, and all races. These two Scriptures illustrate this truth. The first Scripture takes place right after the rapture, so it's a good description of the people raptured. The second Scripture takes place after the rapture, during the tribulation, and it's a good description of people saved during the tribulation.

> One of the elders said to me, "Don't weep. Behold, the Lion who is of the tribe of Judah, the Root of David, has overcome: he who opens the book and its seven seals." ... They sang a new song, saying, "You are worthy to take the book and to open its seals: for you were killed, and bought us for God with your blood out of every tribe, language, people, and nation." (Revelation 5:5, 9)

> After these things I looked, and behold, a great multitude, which no man could count, out of every nation and of all tribes, peoples, and languages, standing before the throne and before the Lamb, dressed in white robes, with palm branches in their hands. They cried with a loud voice, saying, "Salvation be to our God, who sits on the throne, and to the Lamb!" (Revelation 7:9-10)

Notice both Scriptures show people saved from every tribe, language, people, and nation. That's a lot of diversity. The people who were raptured aren't all going to look a particular way. They're all going to look different.

Now just because someone dresses a certain way doesn't mean they subscribe to a particular religion. If you had a neighbor that you swore was Muslim because she wore a hijab over her hair, that doesn't necessarily mean she followed the Muslim faith. She may have worn it for any number of reasons like cultural acceptance, tradition, or even because she liked it. If the person was raptured, I can tell you that means they believed God's truth about Jesus. Anyone who calls on his name will be saved. It doesn't matter what they believed beforehand.

> If you will confess with your mouth that Jesus is Lord, and believe in your heart that God raised him from the dead, you will be saved. For with the heart, one believes resulting in righteousness; and with the mouth confession is made resulting in salvation. For the Scripture says, "Whoever believes in him will not be disappointed." For there is no distinction between Jew and Greek; for the same Lord is Lord of all, and is rich to all who call on him. For, "Whoever will call on the name of the Lord will be saved." (Romans 10:9-13)

8.2.2. Babies And Little Children?

You're likely wondering why the babies and little children were taken if they hadn't placed their faith in Jesus. You're thinking they were clearly too young to make a decision like that. Now the Bible doesn't speak about this specifically, so I'm making an educated guess that this has happened. The Bible tells us that everyone is born a sinner and we all require a savior.

> When Adam sinned, sin entered the world. Adam's sin brought death, so death spread to everyone, for everyone sinned. ... Yes, Adam's one sin brings condemnation for everyone, but Christ's one act of righteousness brings a right relationship with God and new life for everyone. (Romans 5:12, 18 NLT)

However, I believe there's an age in which Jesus holds us accountable to understanding the gospel. That age likely differs for each person based on how

God uniquely made each of us. If babies and little children were raptured, it's because God didn't hold them accountable for understanding the gospel.

Let's consider what the Bible says regarding children. King David's first child died shortly after being born. We learn that he knew that child was with God in heaven because he was confident that he would see him again. This little baby wasn't held accountable for believing or having faith.

> But when David saw that his servants were whispering together, David perceived that the child was dead; and David said to his servants, "Is the child dead?" They said, "He is dead." Then David arose from the earth, and washed, and anointed himself, and changed his clothing; and he came into Yahweh's house, and worshiped. Then he came to his own house; and when he requested, they set bread before him, and he ate. Then his servants said to him, "What is this that you have done? You fasted and wept for the child while he was alive, but when the child was dead, you rose up and ate bread." He said, "While the child was yet alive, I fasted and wept; for I said, 'Who knows whether Yahweh will not be gracious to me, that the child may live?' But now he is dead, why should I fast? Can I bring him back again? I will go to him, but he will not return to me." (2 Samuel 12:19-23)

In the Bible, we also learn that God has a Book of Life in which he writes each person's name.

> Your eyes saw my body. In your book they were all written, the days that were ordained for me, when as yet there were none of them. (Psalm 139:16)

God blots out a person's name when they've hardened their heart against God and refuse to believe in the saving grace of Jesus. In the first Scripture, Jesus is speaking. And the last Scripture was written by King David.

> He who overcomes will be arrayed in white garments, and I will in no way blot his name out of the book of life, and I will confess his name before my Father, and before his angels. (Revelation 3:5)

> Moses returned to Yahweh, and said, "Oh, this people have sinned a great sin, and have made themselves gods of gold. Yet now, if you will, forgive their sin—and if not, please blot me out of your book which you have written." Yahweh said to Moses, "Whoever has sinned against me, I will blot him out of my book." (Exodus 32:31-33)

> Draw near to my soul and redeem it. Ransom me because of my enemies. ... For they persecute him whom you have wounded. They tell of the sorrow of those whom you have hurt. Charge them with crime upon crime. Don't let them come into your righteousness. Let them be blotted out of the book of life, and not be written with the righteous. (Psalm 69:18, 26-28)

This tells us everyone initially starts out in the Book of Life. It's only when we're able to reject God that we're removed from it. Babies and little children certainly aren't able to reject God.

So at what age are children held accountable? The Bible doesn't say. It does tell us that children will be able to eat solid food before they are able to refuse evil.

> By the time this child is old enough to choose what is right and reject what is wrong, he will be eating yogurt and honey. (Isaiah 7:15 NLT)

When Moses delivered the Israelites from the bondage of Egypt and they were headed to the promised land, we learn that little children who had no knowledge of good or evil got to enter that promised land.

> Also Yahweh was angry with me for your sakes, saying, "You also shall not go in there. Joshua the son of Nun, who stands before you, shall go in there. Encourage him, for he shall cause Israel to inherit it. Moreover your little ones, whom you said would be captured or killed, your children, who today have no knowledge of good or evil, shall go in there. I will give it to them, and they shall possess it." (Deuteronomy 1:37-39)

Then during Jesus's ministry he told us to let the little children come to him, for heaven belongs to them.

> But Jesus said, "Allow the little children, and don't forbid them to come to me; for the Kingdom of Heaven belongs to ones like these." (Matthew 19:14)

Take comfort in knowing that any little child that disappeared during the rapture is now with our heavenly Father.

8.2.3. People Who Were Clearly Evil?

You may be having a hard time believing God only took the Christians in the rapture because criminals, murderers, rapists, and such are among the vanished. So why would God take them? Or what really happened? It couldn't have been God's rapture.

God took or raptured everyone who put their salvation faith in Jesus. That means they believed God sent Jesus, his son, to earth to die for their sins and that afterwards God raised him from the dead. Jesus died for everyone's sins and for all sins. That includes the sins of criminals, murderers, rapists, you name it. There is no sin that's too great for Jesus to overcome. There is no person, no matter what they've done who is beyond the saving grace of Jesus. God loves everyone and sent Jesus to die for everyone.

The apostle Paul explains this to us. He lists all sorts of sinful people and then says the most important thing: "some of you were such," "but you were justified in the name of the Lord Jesus." Paul even said that he was the worst of sinners, and he knew that Jesus also died for him.

> Or don't you know that the unrighteous will not inherit God's Kingdom? Don't be deceived. Neither the sexually immoral, nor idolaters, nor adulterers, nor male prostitutes, nor homosexuals, nor thieves, nor covetous, nor drunkards, nor slanderers, nor extortionists, will inherit God's Kingdom. Some of you were such, but you were washed. But you were sanctified. But you were justified in the name of the Lord Jesus, and in the Spirit of our God. (1 Corinthians 6:9-11)

> Although I used to be a blasphemer, a persecutor, and insolent. However, I obtained mercy, because I did it ignorantly in unbelief. The grace of our Lord abounded exceedingly with faith and love which is in Christ Jesus. The saying is faithful and worthy of all acceptance, that Christ Jesus came into the world to save sinners, of whom I am chief. (1 Timothy 1:13-15)

If God raptured someone labeled a criminal, murderer, or such, then like the apostle Paul, that was what they once were. They came to know Jesus and believe that he died for their sins.

8.2.4. People Who Didn't Act Like Christians?

Anyone who vanished was taken by God because they were a believer in the work that Jesus did to save them. Unfortunately, people who've put their faith in Jesus often don't act like it. That's because we're all sinners; it's our nature. The apostle Paul spoke about this war within believers; the desire to do good vs our sinful nature.

> For I know that in me, that is, in my flesh, dwells no good thing. For desire is present with me, but

I don't find it doing that which is good. For the good which I desire, I don't do; but the evil which I don't desire, that I practice. But if what I don't desire, that I do, it is no more I that do it, but sin which dwells in me. I find then the law that, to me, while I desire to do good, evil is present. For I delight in God's law after the inward person, but I see a different law in my members, warring against the law of my mind, and bringing me into captivity under the law of sin which is in my members. What a wretched man I am! Who will deliver me out of the body of this death? I thank God through Jesus Christ, our Lord! So then with the mind, I myself serve God's law, but with the flesh, sin's law. (Romans 7:18-25)

But I say, walk by the Spirit, and you won't fulfill the lust of the flesh. For the flesh lusts against the Spirit, and the Spirit against the flesh; and these are contrary to one another, that you may not do the things that you desire. (Galatians 5:16-17)

Believers have the Holy Spirit from Jesus living inside of them, helping them learn about God, and helping them love others unconditionally. But believers still sin. We all live in a fallen, sinful world, and it's easy to get caught up in worldly ways. It takes hard work and discipline to walk in the light with God every day.

It's unfortunate that the person you're thinking of who was raptured didn't show you Jesus's love. I pray that you don't hold it against them or let it deter you from understanding God's love and saving grace yourself.

8.3. Why Weren't These People Raptured?

8.3.1. Some Christians?

There are many reasons someone may refer to him or herself as a Christian. It could be because their family is Christian, they went to church sometimes, or they did a bunch of works in Jesus's name. If the person is left behind, I can tell you that they hadn't placed their faith in Jesus Christ before the rapture. They didn't have that personal relationship with him that's required. They weren't born again.

Jesus warned people about this. He said it takes more than doing good things in his name to get into heaven. Jesus has to know you. That means his Holy Spirit has to dwell inside of you. That only happens once you've placed your faith in him. See Matthew 7:21-23 in Chapter 8.1.7.

These people were left behind because they didn't believe what the apostle Paul tells us here about Jesus.

> Now I declare to you, brothers, the Good News which I preached to you, which also you received, in which you also stand, by which also you are saved, if you hold firmly the word which I preached to you—unless you believed in vain. For I delivered to you first of all that which I also received: that Christ died for our sins according to the Scriptures, that he was buried, that he was raised on the third day according to the Scriptures, and that he appeared to Cephas, then to the twelve. Then he appeared to over five hundred brothers at once, most of whom remain until now, but some have also fallen asleep. Then he appeared to James, then to all the apostles, and last of all, as to the child born at the wrong time, he appeared to me also. (1 Corinthians 15:1-8)

8.3.2. Some Christian Preachers?

Oh, this is rather unfortunate. Christian pastors and preachers are likely people who've read and studied the Word of God. Most are quite knowledgeable about the Scriptures. Those who are left behind may have gotten caught up in following the law instead of believing in the saving grace of Jesus. They didn't ever ask Jesus to forgive them and come into their life. It's just like this warning we've read before that Jesus gave the people. He said some people who did mighty works in his name like prophesying and casting out demons wouldn't enter heaven because Jesus didn't know them. Now we know that Jesus knows everything, so he meant he didn't have a relationship with these people. His Holy Spirit didn't reside in them. See Matthew 7:21-23 in Chapter 8.1.7.

This is exactly what happened to the Pharisees and Sadducees during Jesus's ministry. They were well studied in the Jewish scriptures. They would have known God's word backward and forward. Some of them even taught the scriptures to their own disciples. Yet they didn't know Jesus or believe in what he did for them. They completely missed the message of the Scriptures because they were focused on earning their way into heaven. Jesus is the one speaking here.

> Woe to you, scribes and Pharisees, hypocrites! For you are like whitened tombs, which outwardly appear beautiful, but inwardly are full of dead men's bones and of all uncleanness. Even so you also outwardly appear righteous to men, but inwardly you are full of hypocrisy and iniquity. (Matthew 23:27-28)

The apostle Paul sheds some light on this for us. He tells us the law, following rules, can't save us. It's only faith in Jesus Christ which makes us righteous.

> Not having a righteousness of my own, that which is of the law, but that which is through faith in Christ, the righteousness which is from God by faith. (Philippians 3:9)

> For what the law couldn't do, in that it was weak through the flesh, God did, sending his own Son in the likeness of sinful flesh and for sin, he condemned sin in the flesh. (Romans 8:3)

If you are left behind, be cautious in listening to anyone who says they were a Christian preacher before the rapture. Since they didn't believe in Jesus before the rapture, they missed God's clear message on how to be saved. I'm not confident they'll be able to explain any of the Bible to you very well. Hopefully they've come to realize their mistake and they've placed their faith in Jesus now. They did a good job hiding this before the rapture, so it's not going to be easy for you to tell if they really are genuine afterwards. So be cautious. Remember that fallen angels can masquerade as angels of light. This person could have the spirit of the antichrist and could be teaching a bunch of lies.

8.4. Are The Raptured People Ok?

8.4.1. What Happened To The People Raptured?

Of course they're ok. They met Jesus in the clouds, and they are currently with Jesus and God in heaven.

> For the Lord himself will descend from heaven with a shout, with the voice of the archangel and with God's trumpet. The dead in Christ will rise first, then we who are alive, who are left, will be caught up together with them in the clouds, to meet the Lord in the air. So we will be with the Lord forever. (1 Thessalonians 4:16-17)

When they were raptured, they also got new bodies that are suitable for heavenly living. They were transformed in an instant and now have immortal bodies.

> But let me reveal to you a wonderful secret. We will not all die, but we will all be transformed! It will happen in a moment, in the blink of an eye, when the last trumpet is blown. For when the trumpet sounds, those who have died will be raised to live forever. And we who are living will also be transformed. For our dying bodies must be transformed into bodies that will never die; our mortal bodies must be transformed into

immortal bodies. (1 Corinthians 15:51-53 NLT)

When Jesus was resurrected, he got a new immortal, glorified body. Here are some things we learn about his body. His body was flesh and bone. The disciples could touch him and feel that he was real. Jesus could also still eat.

> "The Lord is risen indeed, and has appeared to Simon!" ... As they said these things, Jesus himself stood among them, and said to them, "Peace be to you." But they were terrified and filled with fear, and supposed that they had seen a spirit. He said to them, "Why are you troubled? Why do doubts arise in your hearts? See my hands and my feet, that it is truly me. Touch me and see, for a spirit doesn't have flesh and bones, as you see that I have." When he had said this, he showed them his hands and his feet. While they still didn't believe for joy, and wondered, he said to them, "Do you have anything here to eat?" They gave him a piece of a broiled fish and some honeycomb. He took them, and ate in front of them. (Luke 24:34, 36-43)

In this account after Jesus was resurrected, we see that Jesus could either walk through walls or just appear out of thin air. Now I'm not sure the people who were raptured will be able to do this with their new bodies, but Jesus could and he's the only example we have of someone with a new body.

> When therefore it was evening on that day, the first day of the week, and when the doors were locked where the disciples were assembled, for fear of the Jews, Jesus came and stood in the middle, and said to them, "Peace be to you." (John 20:19)

8.4.2. Where Are The Raptured People And What Are They Doing?

The people who were raptured are currently in heaven with God and Jesus. The Bible tells us there are a couple events that happen for them right after the rapture. The bema seat judgment and the wedding feast.

One of the first events that happens for them in heaven is the bema seat judgment. This is a time of rewards. The Bible tells us that we'll all be judged for what we've done on earth. For those who've put their faith in Jesus, there isn't any judgment of sins because Jesus took that on himself. Instead there's a judgment of works where treasure and crowns can be earned. Below, you'll see a crown that some of the raptured people earned, the crown of righteousness.

> From now on, the crown of righteousness is stored up for me, which the Lord, the righteous judge, will give to me on that day; and not to me only, but also to all those who have loved his appearing. (2 Timothy 4:8)

> But if anyone builds on the foundation with gold, silver, costly stones, wood, hay, or stubble, each man's work will be revealed. For the Day will declare it, because it is revealed in fire; and the fire itself will test of work what sort each man's work is. If any man's work remains which he built on it, he will receive a reward. If any man's work is burned, he will suffer loss, but he himself will be saved, but as through fire. (1 Corinthians 3:12-15)

In the Bible, the people who were raptured are often called the bride of Christ. Marriage on earth is meant to be an example of our relationship with Jesus. On earth, we have the closest, most intimate relationship with our spouse. That's the same type of relationship we should have with Jesus, one that's close and intimate. The wedding feast in heaven is celebrating that relationship with Jesus. Only the people who put their faith in Jesus before the rapture get included in this special event. In the second

Scripture below, the "Lamb" is a reference to Jesus and "his wife" are the believers who were raptured or resurrected at the rapture.

> For I married you to one husband, that I might present you as a pure virgin to Christ. (2 Corinthians 11:2)

> "Let's rejoice and be exceedingly glad, and let's give the glory to him. For the wedding of the Lamb has come, and his wife has made herself ready." It was given to her that she would array herself in bright, pure, fine linen: for the fine linen is the righteous acts of the saints. (Revelation 19:7-8)

8.4.3. Are The Raptured People Watching Us?

The bigger question here is can people who died see me or at least know what's happening on earth? The Bible gives us several examples we can learn from. We know there's joy in heaven when a sinner repents. This implies that the people in heaven know when someone puts their faith in Jesus. In this Scripture, Jesus is the one speaking about this joy in heaven.

> I tell you that even so there will be more joy in heaven over one sinner who repents, than over ninety-nine righteous people who need no repentance. Or what woman, if she had ten drachma coins, if she lost one drachma coin, wouldn't light a lamp, sweep the house, and seek diligently until she found it? When she has found it, she calls together her friends and neighbors, saying, "Rejoice with me, for I have found the drachma which I had lost." Even so, I tell you, there is joy in the presence of the angels of God over one sinner repenting. (Luke 15:7-10)

We also see that people who die after the rapture, during the tribulation period who put their faith in Jesus, ask God when he's going to avenge their death and judge the people on the earth. This implies that those people in heaven know that God hasn't avenged them yet. The "Lamb" refers to Jesus.

> When he opened the fifth seal, I saw underneath the altar the souls of those who had been killed for the Word of God, and for the testimony of the Lamb which they had. They cried with a loud voice, saying, "How long, Master, the holy and true, until you judge and avenge our blood on those who dwell on the earth?" (Revelation 6:9-10)

In another example, we see the entire population of heaven rejoicing over the destruction of the city of Babylon shortly before Jesus's second coming. The "great prostitute" is a reference to that city. This tells us that everyone in heaven is aware of some events that happen on earth.

> After these things I heard something like a loud voice of a great multitude in heaven, saying, "Hallelujah! Salvation, power, and glory belong to our God; for his judgments are true and righteous. For he has judged the great prostitute, who corrupted the earth with her sexual immorality, and he has avenged the blood of his servants at her hand." A second said, "Hallelujah! Her smoke goes up forever and ever." (Revelation 19:1-3)

The last example I'll provide is a conversation between King Saul and a dead prophet of God, Samuel. King Saul had rebelled against God and wasn't getting answers from God through his prophets or dreams, so he found a psychic whom he used to commune with the dead. Yes, he really did that. Let's see how it happened.

> When Saul inquired of Yahweh, Yahweh didn't answer him by dreams, by Urim, or by prophets. Then Saul said to his servants, "Seek for me a

woman who has a familiar spirit, that I may go to her and inquire of her." His servants said to him, "Behold, there is a woman who has a familiar spirit at Endor." ... Then the woman said, "Whom shall I bring up to you?" He said, "Bring Samuel up for me." ... He said to her, "What does he look like?" She said, "An old man comes up. He is covered with a robe." Saul perceived that it was Samuel, and he bowed with his face to the ground, and showed respect. Samuel said to Saul, "Why have you disturbed me, to bring me up?" Saul answered, "I am very distressed; for the Philistines make war against me, and God has departed from me, and answers me no more, by prophets, or by dreams. Therefore I have called you, that you may make known to me what I shall do." Samuel said, "Why then do you ask me, since Yahweh has departed from you and has become your adversary? Yahweh has done to you as he spoke by me. Yahweh has torn the kingdom out of your hand and given it to your neighbor, even to David. Because you didn't obey Yahweh's voice, and didn't execute his fierce wrath on Amalek, therefore Yahweh has done this thing to you today. Moreover Yahweh will deliver Israel also with you into the hand of the Philistines; and tomorrow you and your sons will be with me. Yahweh will deliver the army of Israel also into the hand of the Philistines." (1 Samuel 28:6-7, 11, 14-19)

In the conversation, we learn that Samuel, the dead prophet of God, knew the Lord had left Saul, knew the Lord told Saul he was going to give his kingdom to David, and knew Saul refused to destroy the Amalekites. What's even more shocking is that Samuel knew Saul was going to be defeated the next day and that he and his sons would die and be with Samuel. Clearly Samuel knew what was happening on earth. But he also had some knowledge of future events that he obviously received from God.

Based on these examples, we can know that people in heaven indeed have some knowledge of what's happening on earth. However, they aren't watching you like a creepy stalker, so to speak. Their knowledge is likely because God or an angel has told them.

8.5. Will I See The Raptured People Again?

Well that all depends on you. If you put your faith in Jesus and believe that he died for your sins, then yes, you'll see the raptured people again. As a believer, if you die before the second coming of Jesus, you'll see them in heaven. You'll die as a tribulation saint; one who is saved out of the tribulation and "great suffering."

> After these things I looked, and behold, a great multitude, which no man could count, out of every nation and of all tribes, peoples, and languages, standing before the throne and before the Lamb, dressed in white robes, with palm branches in their hands. ... One of the elders answered, saying to me, "These who are arrayed in the white robes, who are they, and where did they come from?" I told him, "My lord, you know." He said to me, "These are those who came out of the great suffering. They washed their robes, and made them white in the Lamb's blood." (Revelation 7:9, 13-14)

If you survive through the tribulation as a believer, then you'll see them again at the second coming of Jesus and into the millennial period during Jesus's reign on earth. In this Scripture, we see what's happening at Jesus's second coming. After Satan gets bound, Jesus separates the believers who didn't receive the mark and didn't worship the Antichrist. They are the sheep. They get to live with Jesus in his kingdom on earth. The people who were raptured will be with him there.

> But when the Son of Man comes in his glory, and all the holy angels with him, then he will sit on the throne of his glory. Before him all the nations will be gathered, and he will separate them one

from another, as a shepherd separates the sheep from the goats. He will set the sheep on his right hand, but the goats on the left. Then the King will tell those on his right hand, "Come, blessed of my Father, inherit the Kingdom prepared for you from the foundation of the world." ... Then he will say also to those on the left hand, "Depart from me, you cursed, into the eternal fire which is prepared for the devil and his angels." (Matthew 25:31-34, 41)

If you choose not to believe, then no, you won't see them again. That's because the raptured people will always be where Jesus is, either in heaven, or on earth with him in the millennial kingdom. When you die, or if you're alive when Jesus comes back, you'll end up in the lake of fire that was created for Satan. In the Scripture above, you are the goat.

Part 3

There's Hope For You

Chapter 9 - How To Be Saved

That's right. There's still hope for you. Just because you were left behind doesn't mean you can't be saved. In Part 1 of this book, I gave you a quick rundown on how to be saved. I'll expand on those truths here.

9.1. You Will Live For Eternity

You can stop your quest for the fountain of youth. Every one of us is going to live for eternity. That's right, you're going to be an immortal. When your body is resurrected it is raised imperishable. It'll last forever.

> So also is the resurrection of the dead. The body is sown perishable; it is raised imperishable. (1 Corinthians 15:42)

God even put eternity in your heart so you would know this truth and you would long to be with him.

> He has also set eternity in their hearts. (Ecclesiastes 3:11)

You even get to choose where you want to spend eternity. The choices are heaven or hell. God created both places, and contrary to what you may believe, he also rules over both places.

> Yahweh has established his throne in the heavens. His kingdom rules over all. (Psalm 103:19)

> Your kingdom is an everlasting kingdom. Your dominion endures throughout all generations.

Yahweh is faithful in all his words, and loving in all his deeds. (Psalm 145:13)

In this Scripture, we learn what happens when Jesus returns at his second coming. Jesus is the "Son of Man" and the "King." He's going to separate the believers from the unbelievers. The believers are "sheep" and the unbelievers are "goats." God and Jesus live in heaven as will those who believe and are deemed righteous. Heaven is called the "Kingdom." As for hell, God created this lake of fire as eternal punishment for Satan and the other fallen angels. Hell was not created for you.

But when the Son of Man comes in his glory, and all the holy angels with him, then he will sit on the throne of his glory. Before him all the nations will be gathered, and he will separate them one from another, as a shepherd separates the sheep from the goats. He will set the sheep on his right hand, but the goats on the left. Then the King will tell those on his right hand, "Come, blessed of my Father, inherit the Kingdom prepared for you from the foundation of the world." ... Then he will say also to those on the left hand, "Depart from me, you cursed, into the eternal fire which is prepared for the devil and his angels." ... These will go away into eternal punishment, but the righteous into eternal life. (Matthew 25:31-34, 41, 46)

Even though God created hell for the fallen angels, it's your default destination as an unbeliever.

But for the cowardly, unbelieving, sinners, abominable, murderers, sexually immoral, sorcerers, idolaters, and all liars, their part is in the lake that burns with fire and sulfur, which is the second death. (Revelation 21:8)

That's because you're either for Jesus or you're against him. You have to actively choose to live in heaven. God gave us clear directions to heaven that are easy to follow. In this Scripture, Jesus is speaking. He says come to him, and he'll give your soul rest.

> Come to me, all you who labor and are heavily burdened, and I will give you rest. Take my yoke upon you and learn from me, for I am gentle and humble in heart; and you will find rest for your souls. For my yoke is easy, and my burden is light (Matthew 11:28-30)

9.2. Heaven Is For Perfect Righteous People

God created everything including you, heaven, hell, earth, and everything in it.

> In the beginning, God created the heavens and the earth. (Genesis 1:1)

Since God created heaven, he made the rules regarding who gets to live there. He's the judge that we're all accountable to.

> It is God alone who judges; he decides who will rise and who will fall. (Psalm 75:7 NLT)

> Nothing in all creation is hidden from God. Everything is naked and exposed before his eyes, and he is the one to whom we are accountable. (Hebrews 4:13 NLT)

God is also the only one qualified to make the rules because he's perfect, holy, and righteous. In him there is no darkness. Every decision he makes is perfect and just.

> There is no one as holy as Yahweh. (1 Samuel 2:2)

> This is the message which we have heard from him and announce to you, that God is light, and in him is no darkness at all. (1 John 1:5)

For I will proclaim Yahweh's name. Ascribe greatness to our God! The Rock: his work is perfect, for all his ways are just. A God of faithfulness who does no wrong, just and right is he. (Deuteronomy 32:3-4)

So what are God's rules to enter heaven? There's only one rule. You must be perfect and sinless, just as God is. God can't even look upon evil.

Aren't you from everlasting, Yahweh my God, my Holy One? ... You who have purer eyes than to see evil, and who cannot look on perversity. (Habakkuk 1:12-13)

Therefore you shall be perfect, just as your Father in heaven is perfect. (Matthew 5:48)

Remember the Pharisees we've talked about in some prior chapters? They were one of the Jewish leadership groups that Jesus often confronted because of their strict adherence to the law. They were trying to earn their way into heaven. Jesus says even their level of dedication to following God's rules isn't good enough. Jesus is the one speaking here.

For I tell you that unless your righteousness exceeds that of the scribes and Pharisees, there is no way you will enter into the Kingdom of Heaven. (Matthew 5:20)

So how on earth can you ever be good enough, ever be perfect? That's the problem. You can't. It's impossible for you to attain perfection by yourself. God knows it's impossible for us too, and that's exactly why he sent Jesus. Jesus is the only one who ever lived who is perfect. That's because he's God in the flesh. God made a way for us imperfect, sinful people to live in heaven. That's by having our name written in the Lamb's Book of Life. Jesus is the "Lamb," so it's Jesus's Book of Life.

> There will in no way enter into it anything profane, or one who causes an abomination or a lie, but only those who are written in the Lamb's book of life. (Revelation 21:27)

You see, God has delegated his decision regarding who gets to enter heaven to Jesus. This is because God and Jesus are one, and Jesus can only do God's will. So Jesus is the judge of your righteousness. In this first Scripture, Jesus is speaking of himself and his father, God. In the second verse Jesus is the one who ordered the disciples to preach everywhere.

> Jesus therefore answered them, "Most certainly, I tell you, the Son can do nothing of himself, but what he sees the Father doing. For whatever things he does, these the Son also does likewise. … For as the Father raises the dead and gives them life, even so the Son also gives life to whom he desires. For the Father judges no one, but he has given all judgment to the Son…. … I can of myself do nothing. As I hear, I judge, and my judgment is righteous; because I don't seek my own will, but the will of my Father who sent me." (John 5:19, 21-22, 30)

> And he ordered us to preach everywhere and to testify that Jesus is the one appointed by God to be the judge of all—the living and the dead. (Acts 10:42 NLT)

And here's the cool thing you're going to learn later in this chapter, Jesus can bestow his perfection and righteousness on whomever he desires to. That's how you become perfect and how you enter heaven.

9.3. Your Problem Is Sin

Even though we all believe we're good people and that whatever bad we've done is outweighed by the good, that's our sinful, human, wishful thinking. We are anything but perfect, holy, and righteous. We're a bunch of sinners.

> For we previously warned both Jews and Greeks that they are all under sin. As it is written, "There is no one righteous; no, not one. There is no one who understands. There is no one who seeks after God. They have all turned away. They have together become unprofitable. There is no one who does good, no, not so much as one." (Romans 3:9-12)

Okay, so what exactly is a sin? It's a transgression of God's law or rebellion against God. When we sin, we've wronged God.

> Everyone who sins is breaking God's law, for all sin is contrary to the law of God. (1 John 3:4 NLT)

You are a sinner. If you think you haven't sinned, you just did by thinking you're perfect. The Bible is full of God's laws and commands. Look at this list describing sinful nature and see how you measure up.

> Now the deeds of the flesh are obvious, which are: adultery, sexual immorality, uncleanness, lustfulness, idolatry, sorcery, hatred, strife, jealousies, outbursts of anger, rivalries, divisions, heresies, envy, murders, drunkenness, orgies, and things like these; of which I forewarn you, even as I also forewarned you, that those who practice such things will not inherit God's Kingdom. (Galatians 5:19-21)

Have you ever lied, been jealous of something your friend has, disrespected your parents, said a cuss word, lusted in your heart about someone, gotten drunk, got mad at someone cutting you off in traffic, or had sex outside of marriage? Those are some other examples the Bible gives as sinful behavior.

Take a look at this Scripture regarding the two greatest commandments in the Bible. Do you love God with all your heart, soul, mind, and strength? Can you honestly tell me that you love your neighbor, which is any fellow human being, just like you love yourself?

> One of the scribes came, and heard them questioning together, and knowing that he had answered them well, asked him, "Which commandment is the greatest of all?" Jesus answered, "The greatest is, 'Hear, Israel, the Lord our God, the Lord is one: you shall love the Lord your God with all your heart, and with all your soul, and with all your mind, and with all your strength.' This is the first commandment. The second is like this, 'You shall love your neighbor as yourself.' There is no other commandment greater than these." (Mark 12:28-31)

We have all certainly sinned!

> For all have sinned, and fall short of the glory of God. (Romans 3:23)

Perhaps this is the first time someone has told you that you're a sinner. If so, then let that sink in for a moment. It's absolutely true, and it's the first truth to being saved. Every single one of us is a sinner.

If you still think you're perfect and haven't ever sinned, well unfortunately we're also all born with sin. We all inherit sin from Adam and Eve. That's right, sin is genetic.

Adam was the first human God created, and then he created Eve to be his helper and companion. They lived in the garden of Eden and walked with God. God only had one rule for them: don't eat from the Tree of the Knowledge of Good and Evil. That's it. Just one rule. God said they would die if they ate from that tree. In these verses, "the man" is Adam.

> Yahweh God formed man from the dust of the ground, and breathed into his nostrils the breath

of life; and man became a living soul. Yahweh God planted a garden eastward, in Eden, and there he put the man whom he had formed. ... Yahweh God took the man, and put him into the garden of Eden to cultivate and keep it. Yahweh God commanded the man, saying, "You may freely eat of every tree of the garden; but you shall not eat of the tree of the knowledge of good and evil; for in the day that you eat of it, you will surely die." (Genesis 2:7-8, 15-17)

Satan, an angel created by God who sinned and was cast to earth, is your enemy. He hates everything God loves. God loves you, thus Satan hates you. Satan knew God gave Adam and Eve this one rule, and he was determined to see them break it. So one day Satan approached Eve and told her she wouldn't die if she ate from the tree. Instead, she'd be like God, knowing both good and evil. In these verses, "the serpent" is Satan, "the woman" is Eve, and "her husband" is Adam.

Now the serpent was more subtle than any animal of the field which Yahweh God had made. He said to the woman, "Has God really said, 'You shall not eat of any tree of the garden'?" The woman said to the serpent, "We may eat fruit from the trees of the garden, but not the fruit of the tree which is in the middle of the garden. God has said, 'You shall not eat of it. You shall not touch it, lest you die.' " The serpent said to the woman, "You won't really die, for God knows that in the day you eat it, your eyes will be opened, and you will be like God, knowing good and evil." When the woman saw that the tree was good for food, and that it was a delight to the eyes, and that the tree was to be desired to make one wise, she took some of its fruit, and ate. Then she gave some to her husband with her, and he ate it, too. Their eyes were opened, and they both knew that they were naked. (Genesis 3:1-7)

Do you see what happened? Satan twisted what God said and flat out lied to Eve. Unfortunately, Eve believed Satan and ate from the tree. What's worse is that she gave the fruit to Adam and he ate from it too, no questions asked. While Eve was deceived, tempted, and sinned, Adam just purely disobeyed and sinned.

Since Adam and Eve sinned, they were no longer worthy of living in the garden with God. God cast them out of the garden. While they didn't physically die that day, death indeed entered their lives. They died a spiritual death because they no longer had the perfect relationship with God. They would also now die a physical death since their bodies would now age. "The man" is Adam.

> Yahweh God called to the man, and said to him, "Where are you?" The man said, "I heard your voice in the garden, and I was afraid, because I was naked; so I hid myself." God said, "Who told you that you were naked? Have you eaten from the tree that I commanded you not to eat from?" ... Yahweh God said, "Behold, the man has become like one of us, knowing good and evil. Now, lest he reach out his hand, and also take of the tree of life, and eat, and live forever—" Therefore Yahweh God sent him out from the garden of Eden, to till the ground from which he was taken. (Genesis 3:9-11, 22-23)

So you see, you inherited sin from Adam.

> When Adam sinned, sin entered the world. Adam's sin brought death, so death spread to everyone, for everyone sinned. ... Yes, Adam's one sin brings condemnation for everyone, but Christ's one act of righteousness brings a right relationship with God and new life for everyone. (Romans 5:12, 18 NLT)

If you still think you aren't a sinner, you are deceiving yourself and calling God a liar.

> If we say that we have no sin, we deceive ourselves, and the truth is not in us. If we confess our sins, he is faithful and righteous to forgive us the sins, and to cleanse us from all unrighteousness. If we say that we haven't sinned, we make him a liar, and his word is not in us. (1 John 1:8-10)

God knows you're a sinner. He knows everything about you.

> Yahweh, you have searched me, and you know me. You know my sitting down and my rising up. You perceive my thoughts from afar. You search out my path and my lying down, and are acquainted with all my ways. For there is not a word on my tongue, but, behold, Yahweh, you know it altogether. You hem me in behind and before. You laid your hand on me. This knowledge is beyond me. It's lofty. I can't attain it. Where could I go from your Spirit? Or where could I flee from your presence? (Psalm 139:1-7)

Even if you still don't think you're a sinner, do you know who else knows you're a sinner? Satan does. Just like Satan was watching Adam and Eve in the garden, he and his fallen angel cohorts are watching you. They've been watching humans for thousands of years. They know our sinful nature better than we do. Satan has been racking up a huge list of sins to accuse you with before God. Remember that he hates you, and he wants to see you get the same punishment that God gave to him for sinning.

Remember in a prior chapter when we saw the conversation between God and Satan regarding Job? Satan had been watching Job. He said Job would curse God's face if he suddenly wasn't blessed anymore. In these verses, "God's sons" refers to angels.

> Now on the day when God's sons came to present themselves before Yahweh, Satan also came

among them. Yahweh said to Satan, "Where have you come from?" Then Satan answered Yahweh, and said, "From going back and forth in the earth, and from walking up and down in it." Yahweh said to Satan, "Have you considered my servant, Job? For there is no one like him in the earth, a blameless and an upright man, one who fears God, and turns away from evil." Then Satan answered Yahweh, and said, "Does Job fear God for nothing? Haven't you made a hedge around him, and around his house, and around all that he has, on every side? You have blessed the work of his hands, and his substance is increased in the land. But stretch out your hand now, and touch all that he has, and he will renounce you to your face." (Job 1:6-11)

Satan and his demonic army make these same accusations against you to God. As this Scripture says, he accuses people before God day and night. In this Scripture, Satan is "the accuser."

I heard a loud voice in heaven, saying, "Now the salvation, the power, and the Kingdom of our God, and the authority of his Christ has come; for the accuser of our brothers has been thrown down, who accuses them before our God day and night." (Revelation 12:10)

9.4. Sin Has Consequences

Our sin problem is terrible news for us because sin has several consequences. God said sinners don't get to live in heaven. This is because sin separates us from God. Remember that you have to be perfect to live in heaven with God because God is perfect and holy. It only takes one sin or iniquity to keep you out of heaven and get your name blotted out of the Book of Life. You should be realizing by now that you have many more sins than just one. You don't deserve to live in heaven because you're a sinner. See also Revelation 21:27 in Chapter 9.2. The "Lamb" is a reference to Jesus.

But your iniquities have separated you and your God, and your sins have hidden his face from you. (Isaiah 59:2)

Yahweh said to Moses, "Whoever has sinned against me, I will blot him out of my book." (Exodus 32:33)

So if sinners can't live in heaven, that means we're destined to live in the other place, hell. This is the worst consequence. God has a punishment for sin. It's eternity in hell, a second death that lasts forever. The second Scripture here is a description of the final judgment for mankind and the dead are standing before "the throne" of God.

For the wages of sin is death, but the free gift of God is eternal life in Christ Jesus our Lord. (Romans 6:23)

I saw the dead, the great and the small, standing before the throne, and they opened books. Another book was opened, which is the book of life. The dead were judged out of the things which were written in the books, according to their works. The sea gave up the dead who were in it. Death and Hades gave up the dead who were in them. They were judged, each one according to his works. Death and Hades were thrown into the lake of fire. This is the second death, the lake of fire. If anyone was not found written in the book of life, he was cast into the lake of fire. (Revelation 20:12-15)

Satan was the first sinner, not Adam. God created hell as punishment for Satan. Hell is where fallen angels and people who are eternally separated from God go. It's where fallen angels and people who are dead to God go. Hell is the eternal graveyard. In this Scripture, we see Jesus at his second coming. He sends the sinners who haven't placed their faith in him to the lake of fire, and he states exactly that. The eternal fire is meant for the devil. The "Son of Man" is Jesus.

> But when the Son of Man comes in his glory, and all the holy angels with him, then he will sit on the throne of his glory. ... Then he will say ... "Depart from me, you cursed, into the eternal fire which is prepared for the devil and his angels." (Matthew 25:31, 41)

You know as well as I do that it's impossible to follow all of God's commands. Sinfulness is in our nature. Since sinners deserve death, the lake of fire, and eternal punishment, we clearly have a problem with the worst eternal consequences.

9.5. God Loves You

Now we get to the great news. God loves you!

> Praise Yahweh, all you nations! Extol him, all you peoples! For his loving kindness is great toward us. Yahweh's faithfulness endures forever. Praise Yah! (Psalm 117:1-2)

God's love for us is so strong that nothing can separate us from it. Not death, wicked fallen angels, other people, our own sin, or anything else. God's love for us is pure, unconditional, and unbreakable.

> Who shall separate us from the love of Christ? Could oppression, or anguish, or persecution, or famine, or nakedness, or peril, or sword? Even as it is written, "For your sake we are killed all day long. We were accounted as sheep for the slaughter." No, in all these things, we are more than conquerors through him who loved us. For I am persuaded that neither death, nor life, nor angels, nor principalities, nor things present, nor things to come, nor powers, nor height, nor depth, nor any other created thing will be able to separate us from God's love which is in Christ

Jesus our Lord. (Romans 8:35-39)

Because God loves you, he created you for heaven so that you could be with him for eternity. Remember earlier, I told you God put eternity in our hearts. It's because God wants us to know where our home is. Our rightful home is with God in heaven. That's where it all started before sin entered the picture. Adam and Eve lived with God in the garden of Eden. In this Scripture, we learn that God has a city prepared for us right now in heaven. Abraham longed to live in this heavenly city that God built.

> By faith, Abraham, ... lived as an alien in the land of promise, as in a land not his own, dwelling in tents with Isaac and Jacob, the heirs with him of the same promise. For he looked for the city which has the foundations, whose builder and maker is God. By faith, even Sarah herself received power to conceive, and she bore a child when she was past age, since she counted him faithful who had promised. Therefore as many as the stars of the sky in multitude, and as innumerable as the sand which is by the sea shore, were fathered by one man, and him as good as dead. These all died in faith, not having received the promises, but having seen them and embraced them from afar, and having confessed that they were strangers and pilgrims on the earth. For those who say such things make it clear that they are seeking a country of their own. If indeed they had been thinking of that country from which they went out, they would have had enough time to return. But now they desire a better country, that is, a heavenly one. Therefore God is not ashamed of them, to be called their God, for he has prepared a city for them. (Hebrews 11:8-16)

Are you looking forward to the city in heaven that God built for you? Don't you want to see it and see the room he's prepared just for you? God's done this for you because he loves you. He made a way for you to rest in your heavenly home when he solved your sin problem.

9.6. God Solved Your Sin Problem

The reason God is preparing a place for you in heaven, even though you deserve to go to hell for sinning against him, is because he solved your sin problem. God made a way for you to live for eternity in heaven. God loves you so much that he sent his son to take your punishment for sin. That's right. God saw your sin, counted it against his son instead, and his son died for you. Because that's the punishment for sin, death. What's more, you're going to learn that God's son is God in the flesh. Let that sink in for a moment. That means God died for you so that you can spend all of eternity with him lavishing blessings upon you. It's hard to fathom a love like God's.

So who is God's son?

Jesus Christ is the "Son" of God. In this Scripture, we learn that God has appointed his son the heir of everything and that God made the world through him. His son also radiates God's glory. He's the "very image of" God's "substance." That means he's God in the flesh. We also see that his son purified us of our sins and afterwards sat down at the right hand of God. God is "the Majesty." All the angels worship God's son.

> [God] has at the end of these days spoken to us by his Son, whom he appointed heir of all things, through whom also he made the worlds. His Son is the radiance of his glory, the very image of his substance, and upholding all things by the word of his power, who, when he had by himself purified us of our sins, sat down on the right hand of the Majesty on high, having become as much better than the angels as the more excellent name he has inherited is better than theirs. For to which of the angels did he say at any time, "You are my Son. Today I have become

your father?" and again, "I will be to him a Father, and he will be to me a Son?" When he again brings in the firstborn into the world he says, "Let all the angels of God worship him." (Hebrews 1:2-6)

Jesus is God in the flesh. Remember that God is all-powerful, meaning omnipotent. God knows everything and is omniscient. God is present in all places all the time, so he's omnipresent. He created everything that exists. He can manifest in any way he chooses: as the Holy Spirit, as a man, as a burning bush, etc. He's not confined to being in one place at a time like we are. He can operate inside or outside of space and time. He created those after all. As God in the flesh, Jesus subjected himself to death on the cross for you because he loves you.

Have this in your mind, which was also in Christ Jesus, who, existing in the form of God, didn't consider equality with God a thing to be grasped, but emptied himself, taking the form of a servant, being made in the likeness of men. And being found in human form, he humbled himself, becoming obedient to the point of death, yes, the death of the cross. Therefore God also highly exalted him, and gave to him the name which is above every name, that at the name of Jesus every knee should bow, of those in heaven, those on earth, and those under the earth, and that every tongue should confess that Jesus Christ is Lord, to the glory of God the Father. (Philippians 2:5-11)

Now Jesus didn't just step out of heaven, land on the earth as a man, and then start preaching the gospel. No, in the Scripture above it tells us that Jesus humbled himself and was obedient. Jesus was born and grew up just like we do. Jesus had to live as we do, subjected to every temptation we are. He had to do that to demonstrate that he's completely obedient to God, perfect, and sinless. This Scripture below is an account of Jesus's birth. It reveals that Jesus wasn't conceived by human means. He was born to a virgin and conceived by God's Holy Spirit.

> Now the birth of Jesus Christ was like this: After his mother, Mary, was engaged to Joseph, before they came together, she was found pregnant by the Holy Spirit. Joseph, her husband, being a righteous man, and not willing to make her a public example, intended to put her away secretly. But when he thought about these things, behold, an angel of the Lord appeared to him in a dream, saying, "Joseph, son of David, don't be afraid to take to yourself Mary as your wife, for that which is conceived in her is of the Holy Spirit. She shall give birth to a son. You shall name him Jesus, for it is he who shall save his people from their sins." (Matthew 1:18-21)

That means Jesus is all God and all human.

> For in Christ lives all the fullness of God in a human body. (Colossians 2:9 NLT)

And what did Jesus do exactly?

Thankfully, Jesus came to your rescue. God sent his son Jesus to earth to live the sinless life that you can't. God then placed all of your sinful behavior upon Jesus and crucified him for it. Jesus had to die because God said the penalty for sin is death. Jesus took your sins and died in your place. Jesus died so you can live with him and God in heaven. Jesus did that to demonstrate how much he loves you. These Scriptures all speak about Jesus and how he died for your sins.

> For him who knew no sin he made to be sin on our behalf; so that in him we might become the righteousness of God. (2 Corinthians 5:21)

> For I delivered to you first of all that which I also received: that Christ died for our sins according to the Scriptures, that he was buried, that he was

raised on the third day according to the Scriptures. (1 Corinthians 15:3-4)

He himself bore our sins in his body on the tree, that we, having died to sins, might live to righteousness. You were healed by his wounds. (1 Peter 2:24)

My little children, I write these things to you so that you may not sin. If anyone sins, we have a Counselor with the Father, Jesus Christ, the righteous. And he is the atoning sacrifice for our sins, and not for ours only, but also for the whole world. (1 John 2:1-2)

The saying is faithful and worthy of all acceptance, that Christ Jesus came into the world to save sinners. (1 Timothy 1:15)

<u>How could Jesus take my sin?</u>
There are a few reasons why Jesus was able to take your sin. First, he's God, and that means he's certainly capable of taking your sin since he's all-powerful and all-knowing. He knew all the sins you were going to commit before you were born. He laid them all on himself.

Second, since Jesus is also fully human, that means he can substitute himself for a human. Remember, he subjected himself to every temptation and feeling that we have. He also had to be human so he could die for us since that's our punishment for sin. In these verses, Jesus is "the Son."

Because God's children are human beings— made of flesh and blood—the Son also became flesh and blood. For only as a human being could he die, and only by dying could he break the power of the devil, who had the power of death. Only in this way could he set free all who have lived their lives as slaves to the fear of dying. We also know that the Son did not come to help angels; he came to help the descendants of

Abraham. (Hebrews 2:14-16 NLT)

Lastly, as a human Jesus never sinned. He lived the perfect life that we can't. He could only do that because he's also fully God. Jesus was our perfect substitute. This Scripture is about Jesus, the "high priest," and how he was indeed fitting for this task.

> But he, because he lives forever, has his priesthood unchangeable. Therefore he is also able to save to the uttermost those who draw near to God through him, seeing that he lives forever to make intercession for them. For such a high priest was fitting for us: holy, guiltless, undefiled, separated from sinners, and made higher than the heavens; who doesn't need, like those high priests, to offer up sacrifices daily, first for his own sins, and then for the sins of the people. For he did this once for all, when he offered up himself. (Hebrews 7:24-27)

In times past, God's people sacrificed animals to atone for their sins. What's more is that they had to sacrifice those animals continually. With Jesus, all of that went away. Those sacrifices are no longer needed. They were just a foreshadow of what was to come with Jesus. Jesus was sacrificed once for everyone.

> For the law, having a shadow of the good to come, not the very image of the things, can never with the same sacrifices year by year, which they offer continually, make perfect those who draw near. ... But in those sacrifices there is a yearly reminder of sins. For it is impossible that the blood of bulls and goats should take away sins. Therefore when he comes into the world, he says, "You didn't desire sacrifice and offering, but you prepared a body for me. ... by which will we have been sanctified through the offering of the body of Jesus Christ once for all. (Hebrews 10:1, 3-5, 10)

It's the sweat and blood of Jesus that saves your

soul. The wage of sin is death, and life is found in the blood. Therefore, in order for the wages of sin to be paid, blood is required.

> For the life of the flesh is in the blood. I have given it to you on the altar to make atonement for your souls; for it is the blood that makes atonement by reason of the life. (Leviticus 17:11)

It's Jesus's blood that washed away your sins.

> But—"When God our Savior revealed his kindness and love, he saved us, not because of the righteous things we had done, but because of his mercy. He washed away our sins, giving us a new birth and new life through the Holy Spirit." (Titus 3:4-5 NLT)

How did Jesus die for me?

I need you to realize that Jesus's death was no ordinary death. Remember, his death is the death you deserve. So it's important for you to understand the full weight of what he did for you. He was crucified. This is one of the most horrible ways to die. The Persians were the first to practice crucifixion, but the Romans perfected it to deliver maximum pain and prolong death. Let's read the account of Jesus's crucifixion by John, one of his disciples who was an eyewitness.

> Pilate then took Jesus, and flogged him. The soldiers twisted thorns into a crown, and put it on his head, and dressed him in a purple garment. They kept saying, "Hail, King of the Jews!" and they kept slapping him. ... Jesus therefore came out, wearing the crown of thorns and the purple garment. Pilate said to them, "Behold, the man!" When therefore the chief priests and the officers saw him, they shouted, saying, "Crucify! Crucify!" Pilate said to them, "Take him yourselves, and crucify him, for I find no basis for a charge against him." The Jews

answered him, "We have a law, and by our law he ought to die, because he made himself the Son of God." ... So then he delivered him to them to be crucified. So they took Jesus and led him away. ... They crucified him, and with him two others, on either side one, and Jesus in the middle. Pilate wrote a title also, and put it on the cross. There was written, "JESUS OF NAZARETH, THE KING OF THE JEWS." ... Then the soldiers, when they had crucified Jesus, took his garments and made four parts, to every soldier a part; and also the coat. Now the coat was without seam, woven from the top throughout. Then they said to one another, "Let's not tear it, but cast lots for it to decide whose it will be," that the Scripture might be fulfilled, which says, "They parted my garments among them. For my cloak they cast lots." Therefore the soldiers did these things. ... After this, Jesus, seeing that all things were now finished, that the Scripture might be fulfilled, said, "I am thirsty." Now a vessel full of vinegar was set there; so they put a sponge full of the vinegar on hyssop, and held it at his mouth. When Jesus therefore had received the vinegar, he said, "It is finished." Then he bowed his head, and gave up his spirit. Therefore the Jews, because it was the Preparation Day, so that the bodies wouldn't remain on the cross on the Sabbath (for that Sabbath was a special one), asked of Pilate that their legs might be broken, and that they might be taken away. Therefore the soldiers came, and broke the legs of the first, and of the other who was crucified with him; but when they came to Jesus, and saw that he was already dead, they didn't break his legs. However one of the soldiers pierced his side with a spear, and immediately blood and water came out. (John 19:1-3, 5-7, 16, 18-19, 23-24, 28-34)

Here's a medical description of crucifixion from a modern day physician, Dr. C. Truman Davis.[1] Jesus's ordeal began in the garden of Gethsemane where he was under so much stress knowing what was coming that he sweat drops of blood. This is called hematidrosis. It's when the small capillaries in the sweat glands break. In this Scripture, Jesus is speaking.

> "Father, if you are willing, remove this cup from me. Nevertheless, not my will, but yours, be done." An angel from heaven appeared to him, strengthening him. Being in agony he prayed more earnestly. His sweat became like great drops of blood falling down on the ground. (Luke 22:42-44)

Next, we read that Pilate had Jesus flogged. Jesus was stripped naked and had his hands tied above his head to a pole. A Roman solider then used a flagrum or flagellum to whip him. It had strips of leather with beads of lead attached to the ends of each. His back, shoulders, and legs were whipped. The strips would first cut through the skin and then into veins. As you can imagine, it caused a lot of bleeding. It literally tore his flesh off. His skin hung in long ribbons. The soldier stopped when Jesus looked to be near death.

> Then Pilate had Jesus flogged with a lead-tipped whip. (John 19:1 NLT)

The cross Jesus was nailed to was shaped like a T. The main beam was attached to the ground. So Jesus was forced to carry the cross beam from the prison to the crucifixion site. It likely weighed over 100 pounds. As you can imagine, he didn't get very far before he was unable to carry it, so a Roman soldier picked an onlooker to carry it for him. Jesus, near death, then walked 650 yards to the crucifixion site. He walked six and a half football fields.

> When they led him away, they grabbed one Simon of Cyrene, coming from the country, and laid on him the cross, to carry it after Jesus. (Luke 23:26)

Jesus was then nailed to the cross. The large iron nails that attached him to the cross were driven through the bones in his wrists. With his knees slightly bent, his left foot was pressed against his right foot and a nail was driven through the arch of both feet. Jesus is now crucified. As he hung there, he would slowly sag down more and more. To ease the excruciating pain, he would try to push himself up, thereby placing his weight on the nail through his feet and experiencing agony yet again. His muscles eventually fatigued. Unable to push himself upward, he wouldn't be able to breath. Then came his final torment as fluid filled the membrane around his heart, crushing it. After Jesus died, a Roman soldier pierced his side, and blood and water came out. Jesus literally died from a broken heart. Here's a psalm about Jesus and this ordeal.

> I am poured out like water. All my bones are out of joint. My heart is like wax. It is melted within me. (Psalm 22:14)

He died on that cross for you. Do you know what Jesus said as he was being nailed to that cross? He asked God, the father, to forgive the people who did this to him.

> When they came to the place that is called "The Skull", they crucified him there with the criminals, one on the right and the other on the left. Jesus said, "Father, forgive them, for they don't know what they are doing." Dividing his garments among them, they cast lots. (Luke 23:33-34)

That horrible description of a tortured death is the death that you deserve. You are the reason Jesus was on that cross. But Jesus forgave you of your sins that put him there! Are you beginning to understand the depth of what Jesus did for you?

Dying for your sins was only half of what Jesus did.

You see, Jesus was only dead a few days. Let's see what happened when women came to his tomb three days later.

> Now after the Sabbath, as it began to dawn on the first day of the week, Mary Magdalene and the other Mary came to see the tomb. Behold, there was a great earthquake, for an angel of the Lord descended from the sky and came and rolled away the stone from the door and sat on it. His appearance was like lightning, and his clothing white as snow. For fear of him, the guards shook, and became like dead men. The angel answered the women, "Don't be afraid, for I know that you seek Jesus, who has been crucified. He is not here, for he has risen, just like he said. Come, see the place where the Lord was lying." ... They departed quickly from the tomb with fear and great joy, and ran to bring his disciples word. As they went to tell his disciples, behold, Jesus met them, saying, "Rejoice!" They came and took hold of his feet, and worshiped him. (Matthew 28:1-6, 8-9)

Jesus conquered death and rose from the grave!

> But God knew what would happen, and his prearranged plan was carried out when Jesus was betrayed. With the help of lawless Gentiles, you nailed him to a cross and killed him. But God released him from the horrors of death and raised him back to life, for death could not keep him in its grip. (Acts 2:23-24 NLT)

Only God has the power over life and death. By doing that, Jesus proved that he is God. He proved that he indeed has the power to take away your sins.

> God promised this Good News long ago through his prophets in the holy Scriptures. The Good News is about his Son. In his earthly life he was born into King David's family line, and he was

shown to be the Son of God when he was raised from the dead by the power of the Holy Spirit. He is Jesus Christ our Lord. Through Christ, God has given us the privilege and authority as apostles to tell Gentiles everywhere what God has done for them, so that they will believe and obey him, bringing glory to his name. (Romans 1:2-5 NLT)

After Jesus was resurrected, he ministered to the people for many days and then departed back to heaven. That's where he's at right now, at the right hand of God. The "Lord" is Jesus.

So then the Lord, after he had spoken to them, was received up into heaven, and sat down at the right hand of God. (Mark 16:19)

Jesus undid the events that started way back in the garden with Adam, Eve, and Satan. This was God's plan from the beginning. Satan is defeated!

Why did Jesus suffer this terrible fate for me?
Love! Jesus, God in the flesh, had the power to step off of that cross and walk away. Love for you is what kept him there. Take a look at this Scripture. Jesus is in the garden of Gethsemane being arrested. It's before his crucifixion. We see Jesus say that he could call more than 12 legions of angels to come for him. Do you know how big a legion is? At that time it was 5,000 men. That means Jesus could have called more than 60,000 angels to rescue him.[2] But he didn't!

Jesus said to him, "Friend, why are you here?" Then they came and laid hands on Jesus, and took him. Behold, one of those who were with Jesus stretched out his hand and drew his sword, and struck the servant of the high priest, and cut off his ear. Then Jesus said to him, "Put your sword back into its place, for all those who take the sword will die by the sword. Or do you think that I couldn't ask my Father, and he would even

> now send me more than twelve legions of angels? How then would the Scriptures be fulfilled that it must be so?" (Matthew 26:50-54)

Jesus didn't need to call any angels to rescue himself. He had the power to save himself if he wanted to. The point is, he didn't. He suffered that terrible fate on the cross willingly. Jesus is the one speaking here.

> Therefore the Father loves me, because I lay down my life, that I may take it again. No one takes it away from me, but I lay it down by myself. I have power to lay it down, and I have power to take it again. (John 10:17-18)

Love for you is what kept Jesus on that cross. There was no better way for Jesus to prove how much he loves you. These verses are the words of Jesus.

> Even as the Father has loved me, I also have loved you. Remain in my love. ... This is my commandment, that you love one another, even as I have loved you. Greater love has no one than this, that someone lay down his life for his friends. (John 15:9, 12-13)

Love. God loves you and wants to spend eternity with you. Remember, he created you uniquely and wonderfully. This is no ordinary love like we humans experience. We love another person because we consider them attractive, and for our love we expect love in return. We tend to put those same attributes on God. That's not how God loves though. God's love is unconditional love. Jesus died for us unworthy sinners. That's how much he loves you. God's love has no bounds. It's infinite, just as he is.

> For God so loved the world, that he gave his one and only Son, that whoever believes in him should not perish, but have eternal life. (John 3:16)

> But God, being rich in mercy, for his great love

> with which he loved us, even when we were dead through our trespasses, made us alive together with Christ—by grace you have been saved— and raised us up with him, and made us to sit with him in the heavenly places in Christ Jesus. (Ephesians 2:4-6)

> For while we were yet weak, at the right time Christ died for the ungodly. For one will hardly die for a righteous man. Yet perhaps for a good person someone would even dare to die. But God commends his own love toward us, in that while we were yet sinners, Christ died for us. (Romans 5:6-8)

9.7. You Can Be Saved

Now that you know what God and Jesus did for you, taking advantage of it and being saved is really simple. All you have to do is believe.

Believe that Jesus is the Son of God.

> Believe that Jesus is the Christ, the Son of God, and that believing you may have life in his name. (John 20:31)

Believe that Jesus died for your sins and rose from the grave afterwards.

> For I delivered to you first of all that which I also received: that Christ died for our sins according to the Scriptures, that he was buried, that he was raised on the third day according to the Scriptures. (1 Corinthians 15:2-3)

> For God presented Jesus as the sacrifice for sin. People are made right with God when they believe that Jesus sacrificed his life, shedding his blood. This sacrifice shows that God was being fair when he held back and did not punish those who sinned in times past. (Romans 3:25 NLT)

Believe that Jesus is the way to heaven because Jesus himself is truth. You can only have eternal life through Jesus.

> Jesus said to him, "I am the way, the truth, and the life. No one comes to the Father, except through me." (John 14:6)

Believe that God did this for you as a gift. It only requires faith on your part. There is nothing you can do to earn it.

> For by grace you have been saved through faith, and that not of yourselves; it is the gift of God. (Ephesians 2:8)

Believe! That's what the criminal on the cross next to Jesus did. That's why he's in heaven with Jesus. Paradise is heaven. Let's look at the conversation Jesus had with both criminals.

> One of the criminals who was hanged insulted him, saying, "If you are the Christ, save yourself and us!" But the other answered, and rebuking him said, "Don't you even fear God, seeing you are under the same condemnation? And we indeed justly, for we receive the due reward for our deeds, but this man has done nothing wrong." He said to Jesus, "Lord, remember me when you come into your Kingdom." Jesus said to him, "Assuredly I tell you, today you will be with me in Paradise." (Luke 23:39-43)

The criminal knew he was a sinner. He knew he deserved to die for his wrongful deeds.

> And we indeed justly, for we receive the due reward for our deeds, but this man has done nothing wrong. (Luke 23:41)

The criminal knew that Jesus was Lord, that Jesus was going to his heavenly Kingdom, and that Jesus had the power to save him.

> He said to Jesus, "Lord, remember me when you
> come into your Kingdom." (Luke 23:42)

You can get to heaven the same way that criminal did. It's not about how good of a person you are, how often you go to church, what church you go to, if you've been baptized, or how successful you are. You just have to believe.

Having faith and believing seems so simple, yet it's incredibly difficult, isn't it? It's hard because our human nature wants to earn it. It's how we get and achieve anything on earth, by our own sweat and blood. But that's not how it works in God's kingdom. Entering heaven is a gift that God has given you. It's not something that can be earned.

> For by grace you have been saved through faith,
> and that not of yourselves; it is the gift of God,
> not of works, that no one would boast.
> (Ephesians 2:8-9)

I know you might not be convinced. I wasn't at first either. In fact, I didn't believe until I was 30 years old. So what changed my mind? I quit relying on hearsay, on other people's opinions and beliefs, and I sought after my own understanding. I started attending church so that I could understand what the Bible said and make my own decision. Over several months, the preacher took us through the book of John in the New Testament. During this time, I learned all about Jesus and what he did for me. By the time we finished going through the book, I was a believer!

That started my journey, but it's God's fulfilled promises that have kept me on this path and turned me from a believer into a knower. That's right, a knower. I don't just believe in God and what he accomplished through Jesus. I know! I know because I've seen that God keeps his promises. I know because I've seen firsthand God answer impossible prayers! Prayers that I've only asked in my thoughts to God.

To live with God forever, all you have to do is accept the gift he offers to each one of us. Jesus, God in the flesh, is that gift. Have you accepted his gift? Do you believe in Jesus and what he did for you?

Do you believe you are a sinner?

Do you believe your sin separates you from God?

Do you want to turn away from your sin?

Do you believe that God sent his son Jesus to take on your sins and die for you?

Do you believe Jesus rose from the grave and reigns with God in heaven?

Do you surrender your salvation to Jesus?

Do you want Jesus to come into your life and help you become righteous?

9.8. The Time Is Now!

I want to encourage you to get right with God right now. There is no better time than the present. Tomorrow is not guaranteed for you.

> Whereas you don't know what your life will be like tomorrow. For what is your life? For you are a vapor that appears for a little time, and then vanishes away. (James 4:14)

> Working together, we entreat also that you do not receive the grace of God in vain, for he says, "At an acceptable time I listened to you. In a day of salvation I helped you." Behold, now is the acceptable time. Behold, now is the day of salvation. (2 Corinthians 6:2)

Don't wait until you aren't ashamed to come to God. Don't wait to fix your problems, get yourself clean, or stop your sinful behavior. You don't have the power to make yourself righteous. It's a battle you will never win. Come to God right now.

> Today if you will hear his voice, don't harden your hearts. (Hebrews 4:7)

He's not ashamed of you. He's not disappointed in you. There's no condemnation for those who believe in Jesus.

> There is therefore now no condemnation to those who are in Christ Jesus, who don't walk according to the flesh, but according to the Spirit. For the law of the Spirit of life in Christ Jesus made me free from the law of sin and of death. (Romans 8:1-2)

It doesn't matter what you've done. He will forgive you. Remember that he loves you unconditionally.

> Bring your confessions, and return to the LORD. Say to him, "Forgive all our sins and graciously receive us, so that we may offer you our praises." ... The LORD says, "Then I will heal you of your faithlessness; my love will know no bounds, for my anger will be gone forever." (Hosea 14:2, 4 NLT)

> 'The LORD is slow to anger and filled with unfailing love, forgiving every kind of sin and rebellion.' (Numbers 14:18 NLT)

Pray To Accept Jesus
If you're ready to believe, then pray this to God. Praying is just talking to God and being honest with him. Say this to God, knowing you mean it from deep down in your heart.

"Dear Lord Jesus,

I know that I'm a sinner. Please forgive me of my sins. I believe that you are the son of God and that you died for my sins. I also believe that you rose from the grave and are reigning in heaven with God. I want to turn from my sins and follow you as Lord and Savior. Please help me by coming into my heart and life. Thank you for making a way for me to live with you in heaven for eternity. In Jesus's name, amen."

9.9. Congratulations! You're A Child Of God

If you believe and prayed for Jesus to enter your life, you have the greatest reward. You are now a child of God!

> Everyone who believes that Jesus is the Christ has become a child of God. (1 John 5:1 NLT)

You've been officially born again!

> Jesus answered him, "Most certainly, I tell you, unless one is born anew, he can't see God's Kingdom." Nicodemus said to him, "How can a man be born when he is old? Can he enter a second time into his mother's womb, and be born?" Jesus answered, "Most certainly I tell you, unless one is born of water and spirit, he can't enter into God's Kingdom. That which is born of the flesh is flesh. That which is born of the Spirit is spirit." (John 3:3-6)

You are also an heir, right along with Jesus. You get to inherit all that God has prepared for his children: heaven and eternal life. In these verses, Jesus is God's "Son."

> And because you are children, God sent out the Spirit of his Son into your hearts, crying, "Abba, Father!" So you are no longer a bondservant, but a son; and if a son, then an heir of God through Christ. (Galatians 4:6-7)

Take comfort in knowing that nothing, absolutely nothing, not even Satan himself, can take this away from you. Always remember who you are now, a child of God. See Romans 8:35-39 in Chapter 9.5. "Angels," "principalities," and "powers" all refer to Satan and his cohort of fallen angels.

God has now sealed you with his Holy Spirit. You have the power of God and of Jesus living right inside of you. Jesus is with you everywhere you go.

We should be to the praise of his glory, we who had before hoped in Christ. In him you also, having heard the word of the truth, the Good News of your salvation—in whom, having also believed, you were sealed with the promised Holy Spirit, who is a pledge of our inheritance, to the redemption of God's own possession, to the praise of his glory. (Ephesians 1:12-14)

Part 4
Don't Be Deceived

Chapter 10 - You're Being Lied To

I mentioned in Part 1 of this book that you will encounter an unprecedented amount of deception and lies. You can combat the strong delusions by knowing the truth. You need to be alert and ask God for wisdom. Read the Bible, question what you hear, what you read, what you're told, and look things up in the Bible. Just because someone says something is in the Bible doesn't mean that it is. And, just because they've quoted a Scripture, it doesn't mean that they've used it correctly. They could be using it out of context or not explaining it to you correctly. Check to see if the truth has been twisted.

Twisting God's word is Satan's age old tactic. He knows the Bible better than any of us. He's had thousands of years to study it, and he's lived through the history it portrays. The first thing Satan did in the garden with Eve was deceive her by twisting God's word and lying to her. Unfortunately, she didn't know God's word well enough to combat his lie. Let's look at what happened. In these Scriptures, the "man" is Adam, the "woman" is Eve, and the "serpent" is Satan.

> Yahweh God commanded the man, saying, "You may freely eat of every tree of the garden; but you shall not eat of the tree of the knowledge of good and evil; for in the day that you eat of it, you will surely die." (Genesis 2:16-17)

> Now the serpent was more subtle than any animal of the field which Yahweh God had made. He said to the woman, "Has God really said, 'You shall not eat of any tree of the garden'?" The woman said to the serpent, "We may eat fruit

from the trees of the garden, but not the fruit of the tree which is in the middle of the garden. God has said, 'You shall not eat of it. You shall not touch it, lest you die.' " The serpent said to the woman, "You won't really die, for God knows that in the day you eat it, your eyes will be opened, and you will be like God, knowing good and evil." When the woman saw that the tree was good for food, and that it was a delight to the eyes, and that the tree was to be desired to make one wise, she took some of its fruit, and ate. Then she gave some to her husband with her, and he ate it, too. (Genesis 3:1-6)

Satan first asked, did God really say don't eat from any tree? Do you see how he twisted God's word? He knew that wasn't what God said. God said they could eat from every tree, except for one. Then Eve added that she couldn't even touch the fruit from the tree in the middle of the garden. She didn't remember God's word very well. Satan finished his temptation by lying to Eve. He told her that she wouldn't die. Eve didn't trust God, and Satan convinced her God was keeping something from her. She decided to believe Satan's lies.

Your enemy, Satan, doesn't want you to know the truth. Here are some delusions you should expect. Realize that Satan will make these lies seem quite convincing. In the first Scripture, "this man" is a reference to the Antichrist. In the second Scripture, the "dragon" is Satan, and the "beast" is the Antichrist.

This man will come to do the work of Satan with counterfeit power and signs and miracles. He will use every kind of evil deception to fool those on their way to destruction, because they refuse to love and accept the truth that would save them. So God will cause them to be greatly deceived, and they will believe these lies. Then they will be condemned for enjoying evil rather than believing the truth. (2 Thessalonians 2:9-12 NLT)

The dragon gave the beast his own power and

throne and great authority. I saw that one of the heads of the beast seemed wounded beyond recovery—but the fatal wound was healed! The whole world marveled at this miracle and gave allegiance to the beast. They worshiped the dragon for giving the beast such power, and they also worshiped the beast. ... Then the beast was allowed to speak great blasphemies against God. ... And he spoke terrible words of blasphemy against God, slandering his name and his dwelling—that is, those who dwell in heaven. (Revelation 13:2-6 NLT)

False power, false signs, and false miracles. The Antichrist's power will look real, but it isn't. It's fake. He will lie about God, about God's name, about God's son Jesus, about heaven, and about the Christians or raptured people who live there. He will speak "blasphemies," which means he'll slander, speak evil of, and vilify God.

Since you're being warned beforehand, you don't have to be deceived.

Chapter 11 - Lies About What Happened And Why

There will be both spiritual and logical explanations for what happened to the millions of people who disappeared and why it happened.

As for the spiritual lies, there will be explanations that claim the people who disappeared were taken to another planet or the mother ship. Yes, I'm being totally serious. They'll say it's because we weren't enlightened and had to be removed. You'll hear them say life will be better without us.

Here's a quote from Barbara Marciniak, a popular new age author, to help you better understand my point. "The people who leave the planet during the time of Earth changes do not fit in here any longer, and they are stopping the harmony of Earth. When the time comes that perhaps 20 million people leave the planet at one time there will be a tremendous shift in consciousness for those who are remaining."[3]

Now some new agers may disagree and claim that we were removed so we could be enlightened and then return and teach everyone left behind. Whether they think the raptured were enlightened or not, this is a spiritual lie. Realize it's part of Satan's new age deception.

Of course, there will be an alien abduction explanation. They'll tell you we were taken for enlightenment, for experimentation, to be a slave race, to help save the earth, or to help save mankind from some apocalypse. Our culture is obsessed with extraterrestrial life. I have no doubt that people have had very real experiences with aliens and have been eyewitnesses to all sorts of signs and wonders as a result of those encounters. The volume of data and evidence we have on these encounters is too overwhelming to refute.[4] However, there's an important truth here that Satan doesn't want you to know.

Pastor Billy Crone has done a lot of research on

UFOs and extraterrestrials.[5] These following statements are a summary of what he's discovered.[6] Aliens lie like demons. Aliens travel like demons. Aliens teach like demons. Aliens communicate like demons. Aliens possess like demons. Aliens are rebuked by the name of Jesus just like demons.

Yes, you read that correctly. Aliens are demons! I don't want you to be deceived about this anymore. I think this is one of Satan's truly wicked lies. It's important for you to be able to recognize this deception and be able to see it for what it really is. We're going to look at each one of those claims in more detail, but first you need to understand what demons are.

The Bible tells us that demons are fallen angels. It all started with the king of demons, Satan. When Satan sinned and rebelled against God, he was thrown down to earth along with all the other angels that followed him, see Revelation 12:4-9. In these Scriptures, Satan is the "anointed cherub" and "Lucifer."

> You were in Eden, the garden of God. ... You were the anointed cherub who covers. Then I set you up on the holy mountain of God. ... You were perfect in your ways from the day that you were created, until unrighteousness was found in you. By the abundance of your commerce, your insides were filled with violence, and you have sinned. Therefore I have cast you as profane out of God's mountain. ... I have cast you to the ground. I have laid you before kings, that they may see you. (Ezekiel 28:13-17)

> How you are fallen from heaven, O Lucifer, son of the morning! [How] you are cut down to the ground, You who weakened the nations! (Isaiah 14:12 NKJV)

When Jesus's disciples were amazed that they could cast out demons in his name, Jesus told them he witnessed Satan falling from heaven. In these verses,

Jesus is "Lord."

> The seventy returned with joy, saying, "Lord,
> even the demons are subject to us in your name!"
> He said to them, "I saw Satan having fallen like
> lightning from heaven." (Luke 10:17-18)

Even though the fallen angels now dwell on the
earth, they still have access to communicate with God
in heaven. In fact, they have to get God's permission
to interact with us humans. Take a look at this
conversation between God and Satan regarding Job.
"God's sons" refers to angels.

> Now on the day when God's sons came to present
> themselves before Yahweh, Satan also came
> among them. Yahweh said to Satan, "Where
> have you come from?" Then Satan answered
> Yahweh, and said, "From going back and forth in
> the earth, and from walking up and down in it."
> Yahweh said to Satan, "Have you considered my
> servant, Job? For there is no one like him in the
> earth, a blameless and an upright man, one who
> fears God, and turns away from evil." Then Satan
> answered Yahweh, and said, "Does Job fear God
> for nothing? Haven't you made a hedge around
> him, and around his house, and around all that
> he has, on every side? You have blessed the work
> of his hands, and his substance is increased in
> the land. But stretch out your hand now, and
> touch all that he has, and he will renounce you to
> your face." Yahweh said to Satan, "Behold, all
> that he has is in your power. Only on himself don't
> stretch out your hand." (Job 1:6-12)

Satan is very real as is his army of fallen angels. A
day is coming in which these fallen angels will get
kicked out of heaven. It happens at the rapture. They
lose their access to God then. There will be a
significant increase in alien (demonic) activity from
that day forward. That's because they will know they

have a very short period of time left. They will be full of rage. You see, they know how this story ends. They will all end up in the lake of fire (Revelation 20:10, Matthew 25:41).

> The great dragon was thrown down, the old serpent, he who is called the devil and Satan, the deceiver of the whole world. He was thrown down to the earth, and his angels were thrown down with him. I heard a loud voice in heaven, saying, "Now the salvation, the power, and the Kingdom of our God, and the authority of his Christ has come; for the accuser of our brothers has been thrown down, who accuses them before our God day and night. They overcame him because of the Lamb's blood, and because of the word of their testimony. They didn't love their life, even to death. Therefore rejoice, heavens, and you who dwell in them. Woe to the earth and to the sea, because the devil has gone down to you, having great wrath, knowing that he has but a short time." (Revelation 12:9-12)

Now that you understand who the demons are, let's consider each of those points about aliens being like demons.

Aliens lie like demons. Aliens claim they are an evolved, higher-educated species. This is the lie of evolution. We know that's a lie because God created everything for a unique purpose. You are not an accident of evolution. You didn't evolve from space sludge. You were created in the very image of God for his glory! Who does God say deceives us with lies? He's the father of lies himself, Satan. He's always on the prowl looking for someone he can deceive. In these verses, Satan is "the devil."

> You are of your father, the devil, and you want to do the desires of your father. He was a murderer from the beginning, and doesn't stand in the truth, because there is no truth in him. When he speaks a lie, he speaks on his own; for he is a liar,

and the father of lies. (John 8:44)

> Be sober and self-controlled. Be watchful. Your
> adversary, the devil, walks around like a roaring
> lion, seeking whom he may devour. (1 Peter 5:8)

Aliens travel like demons. Aliens try to make us think they are an advanced species because of how they travel. UFOs and aliens often appear out of thin air, like they came from another dimension. There are all sorts of sightings of flying saucers and other high tech looking vehicles that seem to appear from nowhere. Who does the Bible tell us has the ability to travel between dimensions? That would be angels. They have access to the spiritual, heavenly dimension, and they have access to our dimension on earth. Remember that demons are fallen angels. In this Scripture, we see that the prophet, Elisha, prayed for his servant's eyes to be opened to the spirit dimension. God opened his eyes, and he saw what the prophet could see, a mountain full of angels with chariots of fire. The angels are indeed among us, we just don't typically see them because they are in a different dimension.

> When the servant of the man of God had risen
> early and gone out, behold, an army with horses
> and chariots was around the city. His servant
> said to him, "Alas, my master! What shall we
> do?" He answered, "Don't be afraid, for those
> who are with us are more than those who are
> with them." Elisha prayed, and said, "Yahweh,
> please open his eyes, that he may see." Yahweh
> opened the young man's eyes, and he saw; and
> behold, the mountain was full of horses and
> chariots of fire around Elisha. (2 Kings 6:15-17)

Aliens teach like demons and promote anti-biblical new age spirituality. These are some things demons in disguise are teaching: people are little gods, people need to worship the earth, Jesus was an alien, sin doesn't exist so people don't need to be saved,

Jesus was really saying that people can become christs, people need to unite in a one world government, and that Lucifer who you know is the devil is really the hero who will save you. A unified government, huh? That's exactly what the Antichrist is going to set up after the rapture. Remember who dwells inside the Antichrist? It's Satan. Do you honestly believe that an evolved species would travel all the way across the galaxy to teach this nonsense and trash talk Jesus? You'd think they'd teach us something useful to solve a global problem, like a cure for a disease. Who does the Bible call out as teaching all sorts of wickedness to people? Once again, it's Satan and the fallen angels.

> Now the Holy Spirit tells us clearly that in the last times some will turn away from the true faith; they will follow deceptive spirits and teachings that come from demons. (1 Timothy 4:1 NLT)

> I marvel that you are so quickly deserting him who called you in the grace of Christ to a different "good news", but there isn't another "good news." Only there are some who trouble you and want to pervert the Good News of Christ. But even though we, or an angel from heaven, should preach to you any "good news" other than that which we preached to you, let him be cursed. (Galatians 1:6-8)

Aliens communicate with us like demons do. Aliens want people in an altered state of consciousness in order to communicate with them. That sounds familiar. That's what new age spirituality teaches with transcendental meditation, channeling, and psychic readings. God's word directly forbids these types of practices and communication with the spirit realm. God knows if you do those things, you'll be talking to demons, and he doesn't want you to be deceived. Now why would an alien want people to do something that God directly forbids in the Bible? Why can't they use a high tech communication method if they're such an evolved species? Because that alien is a demon who hates you, who wants you to sin, and who doesn't want you to know God's truth.

> When you have come into the land which Yahweh your God gives you, you shall not learn to imitate the abominations of those nations. There shall not be found with you anyone who makes his son or his daughter to pass through the fire, one who uses divination, one who tells fortunes, or an enchanter, or a sorcerer, or a charmer, or someone who consults with a familiar spirit, or a wizard, or a necromancer. For whoever does these things is an abomination to Yahweh. Because of these abominations, Yahweh your God drives them out from before you. (Deuteronomy 18:9-12)

Aliens possess people just like demons do. Pastor Crone shares an alien encounter in which a man was possessed by an alien he saw on his property.[7] Witnesses said the man began growling, flailing his arms, and the smell of sulfur was present. Guess who else desires to possess people? The demons do! Jesus and the disciples even cast demons out of people who were possessed. In the first Scripture, Jesus is the one who casts out the demon. The second Scripture is Jesus speaking about an unclean spirit.

> When evening came, they brought to him many possessed with demons. He cast out the spirits with a word, and healed all who were sick. (Matthew 8:16)

> When an unclean spirit has gone out of a man, he passes through waterless places seeking rest, and doesn't find it. Then he says, "I will return into my house from which I came;" and when he has come back, he finds it empty, swept, and put in order. Then he goes and takes with himself seven other spirits more evil than he is, and they enter in and dwell there. The last state of that man becomes

worse than the first. Even so will it be also to this evil generation. (Matthew 12:43-45)

The demon possessed people in the Bible also acted out and inflicted harm on themselves. The demons follow Satan who is a murderer. They want to hurt you. And guess who smells like sulfur? That's right, the demons do! Their abode is hell, the lake of fire, which smells like sulfur, see Revelation 20:10. In this Scripture, we see a "man with an unclean spirit" approach Jesus. That means he was possessed by the unclean spirit.

> When he had come out of the boat, immediately a man with an unclean spirit met him out of the tombs. He lived in the tombs. Nobody could bind him any more, not even with chains, because he had been often bound with fetters and chains, and the chains had been torn apart by him, and the fetters broken in pieces. Nobody had the strength to tame him. Always, night and day, in the tombs and in the mountains, he was crying out, and cutting himself with stones. When he saw Jesus from afar, he ran and bowed down to him, and crying out with a loud voice, he said, "What have I to do with you, Jesus, you Son of the Most High God? I adjure you by God, don't torment me." For he said to him, "Come out of the man, you unclean spirit!" He asked him, "What is your name?" He said to him, "My name is Legion, for we are many." ... They came to Jesus, and saw him who had been possessed by demons sitting, clothed, and in his right mind, even him who had the legion; and they were afraid. (Mark 5:2-9, 15)

Many people who have had alien encounters have seen real, physical beings. We've all seen pictures of the gray aliens and the little green men. Did you know that angels can take on a physical appearance?

Don't forget to show hospitality to strangers, for

in doing so, some have entertained angels without knowing it. (Hebrews 13:2)

For such men are false apostles, deceitful workers, masquerading as Christ's apostles. And no wonder, for even Satan masquerades as an angel of light. It is no great thing therefore if his servants also masquerade as servants of righteousness, whose end will be according to their works. (2 Corinthians 11:13-15)

The two angels came to Sodom at evening. Lot sat in the gate of Sodom. Lot saw them, and rose up to meet them. He bowed himself with his face to the earth. (Genesis 19:1)

Aliens are rebuked by the name of Jesus. Here's what alien abduction investigator Joe Jordan has to say about people who've experienced abductions: "Through the research into the case testimonies it was found that some of the experiencers were able to stop or terminate the experience. There was a recognized commonality in the method that was used among the Christian experiencers. The experience was shown to be able to be stopped or terminated by calling on the name and authority of Jesus Christ. Not as a magic word but by their allegiance to and personal relationship with Him." He has over one hundred testimonies posted on his website.[8] Well that's interesting, isn't it? Now why on earth would an alien respond to the authority of Jesus Christ? Because it's a demon! All the angels are under Jesus's authority.

In the synagogue there was a man who had a spirit of an unclean demon, and he cried out with a loud voice, saying, "Ah! what have we to do with you, Jesus of Nazareth? Have you come to destroy us? I know who you are: the Holy One of God!" Jesus rebuked him, saying, "Be silent, and come out of him!" When the demon had thrown him down in the middle of them, he came out of him, having done him no harm. Amazement came on all, and they spoke together, one with another, saying, "What is this word? For with authority and power he commands the unclean spirits, and they come out!" (Luke 4:33-36)

As we were going to prayer, a certain girl having a spirit of divination met us, who brought her masters much gain by fortune telling. Following Paul and us, she cried out, "These men are servants of the Most High God, who proclaim to us a way of salvation!" She was doing this for many days. But Paul, becoming greatly annoyed, turned and said to the spirit, "I command you in the name of Jesus Christ to come out of her!" It came out that very hour. (Acts 16:16-18)

Jesus Christ, who is at the right hand of God, having gone into heaven, angels and authorities and powers being made subject to him. (1 Peter 3:21-22)

Aliens want people to worship them. Aliens have the same goals as Satan, and Satan wants to be like God. More than anything, these aliens want to be worshiped. We've done exactly that haven't we? Look at how we've glorified them in our culture through movies and books. Do you know what movie currently ranks fourth on the United States all time inflation adjusted domestic box office? It's *E.T.: The Extra-Terrestrial*. It came out in 1982 and has earned nearly 1.3 billion dollars.[9] Look at how many false religions we've created so people can worship aliens. As of August 2019, two million people have said they're attending the Storm Area 51 event in Nevada in the fall of 2019 and another 1.4 million are interested.[10] Two million people. That's equivalent to the entire metropolitan area of Indianapolis.[11] A lot of people are obsessed with aliens.

This Scripture is speaking of Satan whose name is "Lucifer." You can see that he desires to be God.

How you are fallen from heaven, O Lucifer, son of

the morning! [How] you are cut down to the ground, You who weakened the nations! For you have said in your heart: "I will ascend into heaven, I will exalt my throne above the stars of God; I will also sit on the mount of the congregation On the farthest sides of the north; I will ascend above the heights of the clouds, I will be like the Most High." (Isaiah 14:12-14 NKJV)

During Jesus's ministry, he was tempted by Satan. Take a look at what Satan tried to get Jesus to do.

Again, the devil took him to an exceedingly high mountain, and showed him all the kingdoms of the world and their glory. He said to him, "I will give you all of these things, if you will fall down and worship me." Then Jesus said to him, "Get behind me, Satan! For it is written, 'You shall worship the Lord your God, and you shall serve him only.' " (Matthew 4:8-10)

That's right, Satan wanted Jesus to worship him. Remember that Jesus is God in the flesh. So Satan doesn't just want to be like God, he wants to replace God. He wants God to worship him. In these Scriptures below, you can see throughout history that people worshiped demons.

They didn't destroy the peoples, as Yahweh commanded them, but mixed themselves with the nations, and learned their works. They served their idols, which became a snare to them. Yes, they sacrificed their sons and their daughters to demons. (Psalm 106:34-37)

Then he abandoned God who made him, and rejected the Rock of his salvation. They moved him to jealousy with strange gods. They provoked him to anger with abominations. They sacrificed to demons, not God, to gods that they didn't know, to new gods that came up recently, which your fathers didn't dread. (Deuteronomy 32:15-17)

Here, the apostle Paul tells us not to worship anything other than God. When we replace God with something else, that something else is indeed a demon.

Now these things were our examples, to the intent we should not lust after evil things, as they also lusted. Don't be idolaters, as some of them were. As it is written, "The people sat down to eat and drink, and rose up to play." ...Therefore, my beloved, flee from idolatry. ... Consider Israel according to the flesh. Don't those who eat the sacrifices participate in the altar? What am I saying then? That a thing sacrificed to idols is anything, or that an idol is anything? But I say that the things which the Gentiles sacrifice, they sacrifice to demons, and not to God, and I don't desire that you would have fellowship with demons. You can't both drink the cup of the Lord and the cup of demons. You can't both partake of the table of the Lord and of the table of demons. (1 Corinthians 10:6-7, 14, 18-21)

Are you still having a hard time believing aliens really are a deception from Satan? Check out what these secular researchers have said.

A famous UFO researcher and astrophysicist, Dr Jacques Vallee, known for his research that inspired Steven Spielberg's movie *Close Encounters of the Third Kind*, had this to say about UFOs in an interview: "The phenomenon comes in an environment of manifestations that include heightened awareness of synchronicities, paranormal sounds and lights and occasionally absurd coincidences similar to those described in the poltergeist literature."[12]

UFO researcher and author, John Keel, said this: "The UFOs do not seem to exist as tangible, manufactured objects. They do not conform to the natural laws of our environment. They seem to be nothing more than transmogrifications tailoring themselves to our abilities to understand. The thousands of contacts with the entities indicate that they are liars and put-on artists. The UFO manifestations seem to be, by and large, merely minor variations of the age-old demonological phenomenon."[13]

Similar to poltergeist. Really? That's demon possession. The truth that Satan doesn't want you to know is that aliens are in fact demons! Demons are fallen angels, just like Satan. Ponder on this truth for a minute and understand the full weight of it. Satan has been deceiving you for a very long time by masquerading around as an extraterrestrial. We know that Satan likes to masquerade around as an angel of light. It wouldn't be hard for him to be an alien. Refer back to 2 Corinthians 11:13-15 mentioned earlier in this chapter. These demons have used the age old trick of wolves in sheep's clothing to deceive you!

> Beware of false prophets, who come to you in sheep's clothing, but inwardly are ravening wolves. By their fruits you will know them. Do you gather grapes from thorns or figs from thistles? Even so, every good tree produces good fruit, but the corrupt tree produces evil fruit. (Matthew 7:15-17)

Well not anymore. Don't be deceived any longer. The people who were raptured were NOT abducted by aliens!

The alien abduction explanation will be a difficult pill for some to swallow, so it's not the only lie you're going to hear. You may hear that the vanished were infected with some contagious pathogen and were taken or destroyed to protect humanity. Perhaps you'll hear the vanished were vaporized by some sophisticated weapon. They'll tell you it was a terrorist attack. It doesn't matter who they say the enemy is: a specific country, God, a disease, or whatever. World leaders will use it as a catalyst to unite the people against this common enemy.

Think this is pretty farfetched? Do you recall the scene in the movie *Captain America: Winter Soldier* where the Hellicarriers were equipped with advanced guns that could kill millions of people instantly? It was called Project Insight. Now imagine that Hellicarrier equipped with weapons that could vaporize people. It would seem like everyone disappeared. Laser weapons that can vaporize objects are no longer science fiction. Check out these headlines.

China's New Laser Gun Can Zap You With A Silent, Carbonizing Beam[14]

The US Air Force Successfully Tested A Laser System To Shoot Down Missiles[15]

The leaders may even tell you that the vanished are part of some secret space exploration project and were relocated off earth. That they're helping determine the viability of another planet. That they were individually chosen based on a complex set of data. That they kept it a secret for everyone's own good. After all, humanity is at stake. We've already got some big companies working on projects to colonize the moon and Mars. These are some recent headlines that show how this lie regarding what happened to the raptured people wouldn't be too hard for the people left behind to believe.

Colonizing The Moon Could Be The Key To Saving The Earth, Says Jeff Bezos[16]

Beam Me Up Scotty! Researchers Teleport Particle Of Light Six Kilometres[17]

You'll also hear lies that seem preposterous. Some will say there's a sophisticated computer AI or a high tech alien race controlling your reality. That you live in a computer generated video game world. It's called the simulation hypothesis, and scientists have been studying this for years. They may say those who disappeared got red pilled just like Neo did in the movie *The Matrix*. If you aren't familiar with that movie, the main character, Neo, swallowed a red pill that woke him up from his virtual reality world. He then discovered high tech aliens were in control, using humans for power, and were keeping the humans in a simulated reality called the matrix. Or they'll tell you that the raptured people were removed from the simulation because of some defect, like we were nonperson characters. I have a horrible feeling many people will try to "unplug" so to speak when they hear this lie about living in a virtual reality. They'll want to follow in the footsteps of the movie hero Neo. This is a purely demonic lie and will lead to the unfortunate suicides of many people.

Don't believe me? Check out these recent headlines.

Elon Musk Says We May Live In A Simulation. Here's How We Might Tell If He's Right[18]

Comma.AI Founder George Hotz Wants To Free Humanity From The AI Simulation[19]

You'll get some glimmers of truth when you hear many leaders tell you that God did this. The lie they'll spew is that God is angry with humanity because we messed up the planet. He had to remove some people so the left behind could fix the planet and thrive. They may even say that God removed the people who weren't spiritually enlightened and were preventing world peace. You'll also hear them say God did this because he loves those left behind. There are two key truths in this lie - yes, God did this, and yes, God loves you.

Here are some headlines that demonstrate how these lies are being proliferated today.

It's Starting To Look Like God Won't Save Us From Global Warming[20]

Empty Half The Earth Of Its Humans. It's The Only Way To Save The Planet[21]

You need to know that God controls the planet. He knows exactly what's happening and why because he's the one making it happen. Don't believe the lie that God isn't in control of his creation.

> In the beginning, God created the heavens and the earth. (Genesis 1:1)

> God has made the earth by his power. He has established the world by his wisdom, and by his understanding has he stretched out the heavens. When he utters his voice, the waters in the heavens roar, and he causes the vapors to ascend from the ends of the earth. He makes lightnings for the rain, and brings the wind out of his treasuries. (Jeremiah 10:12-13)

> Yahweh has his way in the whirlwind and in the storm, and the clouds are the dust of his feet. He rebukes the sea, and makes it dry, and dries up all the rivers. ... The mountains quake before him, and the hills melt away. The earth trembles at his presence, yes, the world, and all who dwell in it. (Nahum 1:3-5)

I'm sure you'll hear even more lies than what I've exposed here. I hope this helps you question what you are told. Evaluate everything against God's word. What you won't hear the leaders and news telling you is what God's word says happened. Those who believed that Jesus died for their sins were taken to heaven in the rapture.

Chapter 12 - Lies About The Economy And The Mark

This leader, the Antichrist, will rise to power during a time of great chaos such as the world has never seen before. The global economy will be in shambles. Millions of people in the workforce and millions of consumers disappearing will do that. There will be massive looting of the now vacant properties and stores. Identity theft will soar to new levels. To solve the many problems plaguing the global economy, the leader will implement a solution that involves a new global currency and strict control over who can both buy and sell goods with that new currency.

You've already learned that the Antichrist will have authority over everyone on the planet. He also controls who can buy and sell with his mark. You see, he forces everyone to get a mark on their right hand or forehead. This mark is what enables a person to buy or sell. Both of these Scriptures are describing the Antichrist who is the "beast."

> Authority over every tribe, people, language, and nation was given to him. (Revelation 13:7)

> He causes all, the small and the great, the rich and the poor, and the free and the slave, to be given marks on their right hands, or on their foreheads; and that no one would be able to buy or to sell, unless he has that mark, which is the name of the beast or the number of his name. (Revelation 13:16-17)

The one world currency isn't explicitly stated. However, it's inferred from his actions. In order to control who can buy and sell, he must control the monetary system. Currency is at the heart of a monetary system. A new currency and way to buy and sell will be implemented shortly after the Antichrist comes to power. I don't foresee this being just another new form of paper or coin money. It's not easy to control those or monitor people using those. And criminals have gotten good at forging those. No, I'm convinced this will be a digital currency.

Perhaps some of you have heard about or read about blockchain technology. It's the record keeping technology behind bitcoin and other cryptocurrencies. Blocks in the chain store digital information about transactions. The blocks are linked to each other so that each block contains a cryptographic hash of the previous block. This makes it very difficult to alter the data once a transaction has taken place. While the popular cryptocurrencies have used a decentralized peer-to-peer network of computers to record transactions, private sector cryptocurrencies are in development and coming soon. This technology is paving the way for a government controlled digital currency that the Antichrist will use as his economic weapon.[22] Have a look at these headlines and see what's happening today.

Facebook's Audacious Pitch For A Global Cryptocurrency[23]

Bitcoin Won't Be A Global Reserve Currency. But It's Opening The Box[24]

Both Facebook and Walmart just recently announced they are developing cryptocurrencies. They are two of the biggest companies on the planet. Facebook has 2.4 billion active users as of June 2019.[25] Walmart has 265 million customers each week across its global stores.[26] Now how many other businesses and in turn their employees and customers do you think Facebook and Walmart work with each day? I'm sure the number is staggering. If these two companies could have such a dramatic impact on how people across the entire globe buy and sell, it's not hard to realize how easy it will be for the Antichrist to roll out a digital currency so that he can track your every move. I can think of no better way to demand the world's worship and allegiance, which is exactly what the Antichrist is after.

I know these solutions seem harmless on the surface, but they are anything but. There was a time in our past when all people on earth came together in one city, with one language, and one economy and built the massive Tower of Babel to reach into heaven. The people defied God's command to go forth and multiply because they decided they could reach into heaven and be gods. Once again, something similar will happen. This modern Tower of Babel will be economic and monetary unity. This time, the global rebellion will be in the form of willingly worshiping a false god who has control over the entire economy. The leader will use the global currency and the strict control over it as his weapon of worship. Anyone refusing to use the currency and get his mark won't be able to buy or sell. He prevents people who are against him from participating in the economy. You see, a global leader and a one world currency will never work in the hands of sinners or Satan.

The Scripture above told us that the Antichrist will require anyone participating in the economy using the global currency to receive a mark either on their hand or forehead. The Bible doesn't give us the details of what that mark entails, but it's likely something high tech, like an implanted chip or bar code. These headlines show us we're not too far from this technology becoming mainstream.

Elon Musk Wants To Chip Your Brain: Is Biohacking About Convenience Or A Shift To The Mark Of The Beast?[27]

I Got The Mark Of The Beast – And It Will Hold My Bitcoin[28]

There is much speculation about this mark because of this particular Scripture. It says the mark is the number of the Antichrist's name, 666. This has sent many people down the path of using Gematria, Hebrew numerology that assigns numbers to letters, to figure out who it could possibly be. There are all sorts of issues that arise with that methodology. What language do you apply the Gematria to? English? Probably not, because the Bible wasn't originally written in English. So maybe Hebrew? But the New Testament was written in Greek. And then what do you do with English names? Do you have to translate them to another language first and then apply Gematria? No, God does not send us down wild goose chases to understand his truth. The Scripture says it requires wisdom to understand.

> No one would be able to buy or to sell unless he has that mark, which is the name of the beast or the number of his name. Here is wisdom. He who has understanding, let him calculate the number of the beast, for it is the number of a man. His number is six hundred sixty-six. (Revelation 13:17-18)

So we need to be wise and be able to discern the truth. As Skip Heitzig mentions in his book *You Can Understand the Book of Revelation*, it could refer to "the ultimate man." God created Adam on day six and rested on day seven. God appointed six days for man's work and day seven for rest. God told people to work the land for six years and then let it rest in year seven. Six is the number of man. Skip says six repeated three times could be an attempt to give man a divine status, like God, since there are three members in God's trinity.[29] That makes sense because we know Satan wants to copy and counterfeit what God has done.

However, the Bible also tells us that God's Holy Spirit teaches believers all things (John 14:26). Since countless people have attempted to discern this, it may be as simple as knowing this will be revealed to the believers alive at the time. Just like the period of 70 years was revealed to Daniel at the right time (Daniel 9).

Whatever the mark is, know that it's demonic and will seal your eternal fate. Taking the mark solidifies your allegiance to the world leader, the Antichrist, and thus Satan. There is no coming back from this. Do not worship the global leader by taking his mark. If you do, God is clear that your eternal fate is hell, an eternal life of torment with all the fallen angels. In these verses, the "beast" refers to the Antichrist and the "Lamb" refers to Jesus.

> Another angel, a third, followed them, saying with a great voice, "If anyone worships the beast and his image, and receives a mark on his forehead, or on his hand, he also will drink of the wine of the wrath of God, which is prepared unmixed in the cup of his anger. He will be tormented with fire and sulfur in the presence of the holy angels, and in the presence of the Lamb. The smoke of their torment goes up forever and ever. They have no rest day and night, those who worship the beast and his image, and whoever receives the mark of his name." (Revelation 14:9-11)

Refuse to worship Satan and refuse to take his mark. Seal yourself with God's Holy Spirit instead. This Scripture is referring to Jesus when it says "in him you ... believed."

> In him you also, having heard the word of the truth, the Good News of your salvation—in whom, having also believed, you were sealed with the promised Holy Spirit, who is a pledge of our inheritance, to the redemption of God's own possession, to the praise of his glory. (Ephesians 1:13-14)

I know that life will not be easy for you by choosing not to use the new global currency and the mark that goes with it. God knows this too. His word says that he will provide for you. Have faith and trust that he will. Seek him first, and he'll take care of the rest. Jesus is the one speaking here.

> Therefore I tell you, don't be anxious for your

> life: what you will eat, or what you will drink; nor yet for your body, what you will wear. Isn't life more than food, and the body more than clothing? See the birds of the sky, that they don't sow, neither do they reap, nor gather into barns. Your heavenly Father feeds them. Aren't you of much more value than they? ... For your heavenly Father knows that you need all these things. But seek first God's Kingdom and his righteousness; and all these things will be given to you as well. (Matthew 6:25-26, 32-33)

You also need to know that there's a good chance you will be martyred for refusing to take the Antichrist's mark. In this verse, the "beast" is the Antichrist.

> I saw thrones, and they sat on them, and judgment was given to them. I saw the souls of those who had been beheaded for the testimony of Jesus, and for the word of God, and such as didn't worship the beast nor his image, and didn't receive the mark on their forehead and on their hand. They lived and reigned with Christ for a thousand years. (Revelation 20:4)

You need to be prepared for this by having the strongest faith you possibly can. You must have faith in Jesus and truly know that he died for your sins. You must wholeheartedly believe that he reigns in heaven and has promised you eternal life for your faith in him. Your earthly body and experience here are just temporary. Have no fear. Jesus loves you. Jesus will give you a glorious, new, immortal body. And when Jesus sees you in heaven, he will place the crown of life on your head.

Chapter 13 - Lies About How To Be Saved

By now, you know that this new global leader, the Antichrist, will lie to you about what to believe and who to worship. You know that he will claim that he is God and demand your worship. You will further hear his lie that you must worship him to be saved. His mark will be tied to this. He will say having his mark will save you.

Remember that Satan wants to be God, so he imitates what God has done. Anyone who believes in Jesus for their eternal salvation is marked by God. God seals believers with his Holy Spirit. The Holy Spirit is God's mark. This Scripture is referring to Jesus when it says "in him you...believed."

> In him you also, having heard the word of the truth, the Good News of your salvation—in whom, having also believed, you were sealed with the promised Holy Spirit, who is a pledge of our inheritance, to the redemption of God's own possession, to the praise of his glory. (Ephesians 1:13-14)

Satan has a mark too. That's the mark of the Antichrist. The mark that lets you buy and sell. This is why you mustn't take the mark. It isn't an innocent tool that lets you participate in the economy. By accepting the Antichrist's mark, you are accepting him as your authority, you are putting your faith in him, and you are worshiping him. Don't sell your soul to Satan.

Look at what God says is in store for people who take the mark: "the wrath of God." Notice how worshiping the Antichrist and receiving the mark go hand in hand. In these verses, the Antichrist is the "beast" and the "Lamb" is Jesus.

> Another angel, a third, followed them, saying with a great voice, "If anyone worships the beast and

his image, and receives a mark on his forehead, or on his hand, he also will drink of the wine of the wrath of God, which is prepared unmixed in the cup of his anger. He will be tormented with fire and sulfur in the presence of the holy angels, and in the presence of the Lamb. The smoke of their torment goes up forever and ever. They have no rest day and night, those who worship the beast and his image, and whoever receives the mark of his name." (Revelation 14:9-11)

This Scripture tells us those who get the mark are deceived. What were they deceived into doing? It tells us. Worshiping the Antichrist, the "beast."

The beast was taken, and with him the false prophet who worked the signs in his sight, with which he deceived those who had received the mark of the beast and those who worshiped his image. These two were thrown alive into the lake of fire that burns with sulfur. (Revelation 19:20)

The only reason people worship someone or something is because of what they're offered in return. Believers worship Jesus because of his love for everyone and the act he did to prove that love. He died to save everyone. By putting your faith in Jesus and worshiping him, he promises eternal life and peace. Jesus promises salvation in return. The Antichrist wants this same type of devotion and worship. He will promise the same thing. He will lie to you and promise you eternal life as well. He will fill you with false hope.

Your prophets have said so many foolish things, false to the core. They did not save you from exile by pointing out your sins. Instead, they painted false pictures, filling you with false hope. (Lamentations 2:14 NLT)

This Scripture reminds us that Satan, and thus the Antichrist, pretends to be an angel of the light.

> For such men are false apostles, deceitful workers, masquerading as Christ's apostles. And no wonder, for even Satan masquerades as an angel of light. It is no great thing therefore if his servants also masquerade as servants of righteousness, whose end will be according to their works. (2 Corinthians 11:13-15)

Here we see Jesus warn people about false christs.

> Jesus answered them, "Be careful that no one leads you astray. For many will come in my name, saying, 'I am the Christ,' and will lead many astray." (Matthew 24:4-5)

Don't be led astray by the Antichrist. You already learned that he declares himself God. You already learned that he seemingly rises from the dead. He will tell you he's Jesus as well, and that he can save your life. Don't believe him! Jesus is the one speaking here and warning you of this.

> Yet you will not come to me, that you may have life. ... I have come in my Father's name, and you don't receive me. If another comes in his own name, you will receive him. (John 5:40, 43)

The twisted lie in play here is that getting the leader's mark, getting Satan's mark, might save your life temporarily. You indeed might survive through the tribulation because you can use the global currency. However, there's a very steep price. The ultimate price. Your soul. What do you gain when you lose your soul? Nothing! You've lost everything.

> Then Jesus said to his disciples, "If anyone desires to come after me, let him deny himself, take up his cross, and follow me. For whoever desires to save his life will lose it, and whoever will lose his life for my sake will find it. For what will it profit a man if he gains the whole world

and forfeits his life? Or what will a man give in exchange for his life?" (Matthew 16:24-26)

When Jesus returns after the tribulation period, the first thing he does is send everyone who has the mark of Satan to hell. Remember the "beast" is the Antichrist and the "Lamb" is Jesus.

> Another angel, a third, followed them, saying with a great voice, "If anyone worships the beast and his image, and receives a mark on his forehead, or on his hand, he also will drink of the wine of the wrath of God, which is prepared unmixed in the cup of his anger. He will be tormented with fire and sulfur in the presence of the holy angels, and in the presence of the Lamb. The smoke of their torment goes up forever and ever. They have no rest day and night, those who worship the beast and his image, and whoever receives the mark of his name." (Revelation 14:9-11)

Only people who've put their faith in Jesus will enter the millennial kingdom that he comes to rule on earth. Anyone who has received the mark of the Antichrist, the "beast," is excluded.

> I saw an angel coming down out of heaven, having the key of the abyss and a great chain in his hand. He seized the dragon, the old serpent, who is the devil and Satan, who deceives the whole inhabited earth, and bound him for a thousand years .... I saw thrones, and they sat on them, and judgment was given to them. I saw the souls of those who had been beheaded for the testimony of Jesus and for the word of God, and such as didn't worship the beast nor his image, and didn't receive the mark on their forehead and on their hand. They lived and reigned with Christ for a thousand years. (Revelation 20:1-2, 4)

In this Scripture, Jesus is the one speaking. His warning is about following people who promise not to kill you. They aren't the one you should fear or have reverence for. Jesus has the power over your soul. "Gehenna" means hell.

> Don't be afraid of those who kill the body, but are not able to kill the soul. Rather, fear him who is able to destroy both soul and body in Gehenna. (Matthew 10:28)

Don't choose your life on earth over eternity in heaven. If you choose heaven, you get earth thrown in for free. Remember that I told you God is going to make a new earth for us after Jesus's millennial kingdom.

See through the Antichrist's lies when he tells you he is Jesus or perhaps the False Prophet is Jesus. Neither one of them are Jesus. Anyone who denies that Jesus already came in the flesh is a False Prophet. Jesus already died for you. He already saved you. Whatever the Antichrist does with his false powers, he cannot save you.

> Beloved, don't believe every spirit, but test the spirits, whether they are of God, because many false prophets have gone out into the world. By this you know the Spirit of God: every spirit who confesses that Jesus Christ has come in the flesh is of God, and every spirit who doesn't confess that Jesus Christ has come in the flesh is not of God, and this is the spirit of the Antichrist, of whom you have heard that it comes. Now it is in the world already. (1 John 4:1-3)

There is only one way to save your soul. You must believe that Jesus, the son of God, died for your sins, conquered death, and reigns in heaven with God.

> Then Peter, filled with the Holy Spirit, said to them, "You rulers of the people, and elders of Israel, if we are examined today concerning a good deed done to a crippled man, by what

means this man has been healed, may it be known to you all, and to all the people of Israel, that in the name of Jesus Christ of Nazareth, whom you crucified, whom God raised from the dead, this man stands here before you whole in him. He is 'the stone which was regarded as worthless by you, the builders, which has become the head of the corner.' There is salvation in no one else, for there is no other name under heaven that is given among men, by which we must be saved!" (Acts 4:8-12)

Part 5
Bible Basics

Chapter 14 - The Holy Bible

The Bible is a book that most people on the planet have at least heard of. However, many people have never read any of its pages. In this chapter, I'm going to introduce you to God's word.

The Bible is the authoritative Word of God. There are 66 different books that comprise the Bible. They were written by a variety of God's prophets over thousands of years. It is without error in the original text. While God didn't physically write down the words, he told the people who wrote it what to say. In fact, the Old Testament books in the Bible mention more than 2,000 times that God spoke what was written. God's words are even directly quoted hundreds of times.

By now, I hope you are coming to believe that God really can do anything. He created the entire universe after all. Since he did that, don't you think creating a book that contains exactly what God needs it to say to each of us would be pretty easy for him? God tells us the Bible is his word. God made sure the Bible says exactly what it needs to say. In this verse, "Yahweh" is God.

> Then Job answered Yahweh, "I know that you can do all things, and that no purpose of yours can be restrained." (Job 42:1-2)

In the Bible, we read that God often spoke to and through people. In this Scripture, we see King David proclaim that God's Spirit spoke to him. God's words came out of his mouth. David wrote most of the Psalms in the Bible. He's telling us the real author behind his words is God.

Now these are the last words of David. David the son of Jesse says, the man who was raised on high says, the anointed of the God of Jacob, the sweet psalmist of Israel: "Yahweh's Spirit spoke by me. His word was on my tongue." (2 Samuel 23:1-2)

The Bible is indeed the Word of God. These Scriptures tell us that God spoke the words to the authors through his Holy Spirit. It's not the opinion or interpretation of any of the individual authors.

No prophecy of Scripture is of private interpretation. For no prophecy ever came by the will of man: but holy men of God spoke, being moved by the Holy Spirit. (2 Peter 1:20-21)

From infancy, you have known the holy Scriptures which are able to make you wise for salvation through faith, which is in Christ Jesus. Every Scripture is God-breathed and profitable for teaching, for reproof, for correction, and for instruction in righteousness, that each person who belongs to God may be complete, thoroughly equipped for every good work. (2 Timothy 3:15-17)

Moses wrote the first five books of the Old Testament. Here's a Scripture Moses wrote describing the Ten Commandments that God gave to him on stone tablets. He put them into the ark of the covenant. "Yahweh said to me" refers to God speaking to Moses.

At that time Yahweh said to me, "Cut two stone tablets like the first, and come up to me onto the mountain, and make an ark of wood. I will write on the tablets the words that were on the first tablets which you broke, and you shall put them in the ark." So I made an ark of acacia wood, and cut two stone tablets like the first, and went up onto the mountain, having the two tablets in my

> hand. He wrote on the tablets, according to the first writing, the ten commandments, which Yahweh spoke to you on the mountain out of the middle of the fire in the day of the assembly; and Yahweh gave them to me. I turned and came down from the mountain, and put the tablets in the ark which I had made; and there they are as Yahweh commanded me. (Deuteronomy 10:1-5)

That's not the only thing Moses put into the ark. He also put the entire book of God's law in there with the stone tablets.

> When Moses had finished writing the words of this law in a book, until they were finished, Moses commanded the Levites, who bore the ark of Yahweh's covenant, saying, "Take this book of the law, and put it by the side of the ark of Yahweh your God's covenant, that it may be there for a witness against you." (Deuteronomy 31:24-26)

That ark is special, and the way God treats the ark should tell us something about its contents. In this Scripture, King David is traveling with the ark when the cattle who were pulling the ark on a cart stumbled.

> David arose, and went with all the people who were with him, from Baale Judah, to bring up from there God's ark, which is called by the Name, even the name of Yahweh of Armies who sits above the cherubim. ... David and all the house of Israel played before Yahweh with all kinds of instruments made of cypress wood, with harps, with stringed instruments, with tambourines, with castanets, and with cymbals. When they came to the threshing floor of Nacon, Uzzah reached for God's ark, and took hold of it; for the cattle stumbled. Yahweh's anger burned against Uzzah; and God struck him there for his error; and he died there by God's ark. (2 Samuel 6:2, 5-7)

We see that Uzzah touched the ark, presumably to keep it from falling. God struck him dead right then and there for his error. Wow! Why did God do that? Seems kind of harsh, right? Well, the ark contains items that are of the utmost holiness to God. In that book of law that Moses put in the ark were detailed instructions regarding the care and handling of the ark. They weren't supposed to be carrying it on a cart and they knew they weren't supposed to touch it. They were disrespecting it. Do you see the reverence God wanted them to have for its contents? It contained the Word of God. That's the honor and respect God wants us to have for him and for the Bible, his living and breathing word to us.

This Scripture tells us many things about the Word of God.

> In the beginning was the Word, and the Word was with God, and the Word was God. The same was in the beginning with God. All things were made through him. Without him, nothing was made that has been made. In him was life, and the life was the light of men. ... He was in the world, and the world was made through him, and the world didn't recognize him. ... The Word became flesh, and lived among us. We saw his glory, such glory as of the one and only Son of the Father, full of grace and truth. (John 1:1-4, 10, 14)

The Word was "in the beginning." It "was God." It's a him, because "all things were made through him," the Word. It's "life." The "Word became flesh" and was in the world. The Word is the Son of God. Well, you know who this is describing. It's Jesus. Jesus is the Word of God.

Jesus even referred to himself as the Word of God. That means the Bible is more than just a book. It's essentially alive. It's Jesus. It gives life to sinners. Think of the words on the page as the breath of Jesus. When you read the Bible, you're spending time with Jesus. You're learning all about him. The things he did, is doing, will do in the future, his character, and his love for you. Marvel at this great wonder: the Bible is more than a book that contains the Word of God; it literally *is* the Word of God.

Jesus often validated the Old Testament as Holy Scripture when he spoke. These verses are an example of that.

> As they said these things, Jesus himself stood among them, and said to them, "Peace be to you." ... He said to them, "This is what I told you, while I was still with you, that all things which are written in the law of Moses, the prophets, and the psalms, concerning me must be fulfilled." Then he opened their minds, that they might understand the Scriptures. (Luke 24:36, 44-45)

Remember that Jesus is truth. He lived a perfect, sinless life. There is no lie in him. That's because he's God in the flesh. Jesus wants us to know him. He died for us after all. In order to know Jesus, we must know the Scriptures. Since Jesus is truth and he is the Word of God that means the Bible is truth as well. Paul the apostle explains in these verses that God speaks to us through Jesus.

> God, having in the past spoken to the fathers through the prophets at many times and in various ways, has at the end of these days spoken to us by his Son, whom he appointed heir of all things, through whom also he made the worlds. (Hebrews 1:1-2)

God wrote the Bible to teach us and encourage us. But most of all, the Bible gives us hope. That's exactly what Jesus provides us sinners.

> For whatever things were written before were written for our learning, that through perseverance and through encouragement of the Scriptures we might have hope. (Romans 15:4)

Chapter 15 - How To Read The Bible

If you are new to reading the Bible, I'm going to be honest with you, you'll find it difficult at first. Before I became saved and had put my faith in Jesus, I really struggled to understand what I read in the Bible. I also struggled to understand teachings I heard from preachers. Now this is coming from someone who excelled in grade school and in college. There's a reason for this that's explained in the Bible. It's described as a veil that's blocking your ability to read and comprehend God's word. Paul the apostle explains it to us in these verses.

> Even if our Good News is veiled, it is veiled in those who are dying, in whom the god of this world has blinded the minds of the unbelieving, that the light of the Good News of the glory of Christ, who is the image of God, should not dawn on them. (2 Corinthians 4:3-4)

I've come to regard it as something like an illusion. Have you ever seen one of those Magic Eye illusion pictures? If you just look at it casually, it's just a picture with a bunch of random patterns and colors. But if you look at it and concentrate in just the right way, you'll see a cool, 3D image. The veil is kind of like that. Remember that your enemy, Satan, doesn't want you to know the truth. He's essentially blinded you to it. If you read the Bible while you've got this veil on, you're not really going to get it.

Because of this blindfold, before you start reading the Bible, you need to ask God to lift this veil and help you understand what you're reading. In this Scripture, Jesus is speaking and encouraging people to ask him.

> Ask, and it will be given you. Seek, and you will find. Knock, and it will be opened for you. For everyone who asks receives. He who seeks finds. To him who knocks it will be opened. Or who is there among you who, if his son asks him for

> bread, will give him a stone? Or if he asks for a
> fish, who will give him a serpent? If you then,
> being evil, know how to give good gifts to your
> children, how much more will your Father who
> is in heaven give good things to those who ask
> him! (Matthew 7:7-11)

In this verse, Jesus tells us he's always knocking
on the door of our heart. We just need to let him in.

> Behold, I stand at the door and knock. If anyone
> hears my voice and opens the door, then I will
> come in to him, and will dine with him, and he
> with me. (Revelation 3:20)

God will indeed help you. More than anything, he
wants you to know him.

> But if any of you lacks wisdom, let him ask of
> God, who gives to all liberally and without
> reproach, and it will be given to him. (James 1:5)

Now if you've already put your faith in Jesus, the
great news for you is Scripture tells us the veil passes
away in Christ. That when you put your faith in Jesus
it's removed. Here's how Paul describes that.

> But their minds were hardened, for until this
> very day at the reading of the old covenant the
> same veil remains, because in Christ it passes
> away. But to this day, when Moses is read, a veil
> lies on their heart. But whenever someone turns
> to the Lord, the veil is taken away. (2 Corinthians
> 3:14-16)

If you believe in Jesus, you won't live under the
veil of darkness anymore. In these verses, "he had
done so many signs" refers to Jesus.

> But though he had done so many signs before
> them, yet they didn't believe in him, that the word
> of Isaiah the prophet might be fulfilled, which he

spoke, "Lord, who has believed our report? To whom has the arm of the Lord been revealed?" For this cause they couldn't believe, for Isaiah said again, "He has blinded their eyes and he hardened their heart, lest they should see with their eyes, and perceive with their heart, and would turn, and I would heal them." Isaiah said these things when he saw his glory, and spoke of him. Nevertheless even many of the rulers believed in him, but because of the Pharisees they didn't confess it, so that they wouldn't be put out of the synagogue, for they loved men's praise more than God's praise. Jesus cried out and said, "Whoever believes in me, believes not in me, but in him who sent me. He who sees me sees him who sent me. I have come as a light into the world, that whoever believes in me may not remain in the darkness." (John 12:37-46)

If you believe in Jesus, that also means you have the Holy Spirit living inside of you. We know the Holy Spirit is our helper and teaches us all things. So you can also ask the Holy Spirit to help you read the Bible. In this Scripture, Jesus is the one speaking.

> But the Counselor, the Holy Spirit, whom the Father will send in my name, will teach you all things, and will remind you of all that I said to you. (John 14:26)

Now that we've addressed the veil, let's go over how to actually read the Bible. Here's how you find a particular Scripture in the Bible. Let's use John 3:16 as our example. John is the name of the book that's in the Bible. The number before the colon, 3, is the chapter number. The number after the colon, 16, is the verse number. So you're looking for the book of John chapter 3 and verse 16. All Bibles have each book clearly labeled and the chapters and verses clearly numbered.

> For God so loved the world, that he gave his only born Son, that whoever believes in him should

not perish, but have eternal life. (John 3:16)

Sometimes in this book, you'll see me reference a Scripture and it'll have an extra descriptor like NLT or NKJV. That refers to the Bible version the Scripture came from. Instead of the World English Bible that I almost always quote from, I chose a different translation because I preferred the word choice or grammar. I wanted it to be easy for you to understand. Here's how John 3:16 reads from the NLT.

> For God loved the world so much that he gave his one and only Son, so that everyone who believes in him will not perish but have eternal life. (John 3:16 NLT)

The books of the Bible aren't arranged in what appears to be a logical fashion. They aren't alphabetical, and they aren't chronologically based on when the events occur either. Instead, they are primarily ordered by the type of literature they are. The first five books were written by Moses, the next 12 books are historical, then there are five books that are poetic, and the last seventeen books in the Old Testament are considered prophetic. The New Testament has the gospel and historical books first, then the apostle Paul's writings next, and it finishes with a few books by other authors.

Many Bibles include reading plans either in the front or back of the Bible. These can help you read the Bible in an order that makes sense to you, like chronologically for example. You can also find reading plans in the popular Bible apps and on Bible reading websites. You can refer to my website, rapture911.com, for a list of resources like these.

I recommend starting your journey in the Bible by reading the four gospel books in the New Testament. So that's the books of Matthew, Mark, Luke, and John. John is my favorite, so I would encourage you to start with that one. Luke would be my next pick because it's easy to read and understand. In fact, many movies that have been made about Jesus follow the text in the book of Luke. The reason you should start here is because first and foremost you need to know Jesus. The only decision that matters in life is who you say Jesus is. Those gospel books are the account of Jesus's birth, life, death, and resurrection. You'll understand how much Jesus loves you and that he died to save you from your sins. After reading this, you'll be fully equipped to make a decision on what you believe.

After you've read the gospel books, it's really your preference on what to read next. Let the Holy Spirit guide you. You might finish reading the rest of the New Testament books, or you might choose to go to the beginning and read the whole Old Testament starting with Genesis.

When you encounter a verse that's difficult to understand, first pray and ask the Holy Spirit to help you understand it. Then read the verse in a different translation. A Bible app is great for this because you can usually show two translations side-by-side. So you can have the NKJV and the NLT version side-by-side for example. This little trick will go a long way in helping you understand the Bible. Sometimes, it's specific wording or sentence structure we get stuck on and seeing it worded or organized slightly different makes all the difference.

When I first started reading the Bible and learning about God and Jesus, I had a lot of questions. I liked reading Scriptures that answered the questions I had. Most Bibles have an index in the back. It's called a concordance. You can use this to look up Scriptures based on a topic. Let's say you read a Scripture about love and want to better understand what it really means to love. Well, go to that index and look up the word *love*. You'll get a list of Scriptures that contain that word or topic, and then you'll be able to go read further. If you're using a Bible app, the search feature is great for this. Just type *love* in the search box.

Be easy on yourself and don't get frustrated if you're having a hard time. Remember that the Bible is the Word of God. God is infinite. I'm convinced we could spend an eternity learning about God because he is eternal. You will get new understanding from the Bible every day you read it. Just keep at it.

I hope this brief introduction to the Bible has helped you realize that God wrote it just for you. Treasure it like you would a love letter, because that's exactly what it is.

> I have hidden your word in my heart, that I might not sin against you. Blessed are you, Yahweh. Teach me your statutes. ... I will meditate on your precepts, and consider your ways. I will delight myself in your statutes. I will not forget your word. ... Open my eyes, that I may see wondrous things out of your law. (Psalm 119:11-12, 15-16, 18)

Part 6
Building Your Faith

Chapter 16 - Faith Questions And Answers

In this section, we're going to explore some questions you likely have about God and faith.

16.1. Why Did A Loving God Do This?

Many of you will think a loving God wouldn't do something that would cause pain and suffering, so you reject the truth that God raptured the believers. Let's look at why God, who is the very definition of love, allows pain and suffering.

We went over reasons why God raptured the people who disappeared in Chapter 7. To sum it up here, it was to protect those who believed in Jesus, discipline those left behind, and ultimately draw people to him.

No one likes to be disciplined. It's painful. However, the purpose is to correct and teach. God's discipline is good for us. It's meant for our benefit. The apostle Paul tells us about God's discipline and "chastening" in these verses.

> For our earthly fathers disciplined us for a few years, doing the best they knew how. But God's discipline is always good for us, so that we might share in his holiness. No discipline is enjoyable while it is happening—it's painful! But afterward there will be a peaceful harvest of right living for those who are trained in this way. So take a new grip with your tired hands and strengthen your weak knees. Mark out a straight path for your feet so that those who are weak and lame will not

fall but become strong. (Hebrews 12:10-13 NLT)

You have forgotten the exhortation which reasons with you as with children, "My son, don't take lightly the chastening of the Lord, nor faint when you are reproved by him; for whom the Lord loves, he disciplines, and chastises every son whom he receives." It is for discipline that you endure. God deals with you as with children, for what son is there whom his father doesn't discipline? (Hebrews 12:5-7)

Pain and suffering draws people to the only one who can provide comfort and safety. That's God. God doesn't want to see anyone condemned and sent to hell for their sins.

But when we are judged, we are punished by the Lord, that we may not be condemned with the world. (1 Corinthians 11:32)

Times of trouble reveal a person's heart. People who reflect on what's happening to them consider how their behavior contributed to their circumstance and feel remorse for how they've behaved. They'll find Jesus there to forgive them. On the other hand, people who aren't sorry for how they behaved and are bitter about the circumstance they're in will further distance themselves from God because their heart will harden. The apostle Paul is the one speaking in these verses.

For though I grieved you with my letter, I do not regret it, though I did regret it. For I see that my letter made you grieve, though just for a while. I now rejoice, not that you were grieved, but that you were grieved to repentance. For you were grieved in a godly way, that you might suffer loss by us in nothing. For godly sorrow produces repentance to salvation, which brings no regret. But the sorrow of the world produces death. For behold, this same thing, that you were grieved in a godly way, what earnest care it worked in you.

> Yes, what defense, indignation, fear, longing, zeal, and vengeance! In everything you demonstrated yourselves to be pure in the matter. (2 Corinthians 7:8-11)

Jeremiah, one of God's prophets from the Old Testament times, is all too familiar with living during difficult times. He was the prophet who warned his people about the Babylonian invasion. He knew what was coming. When Nebuchadnezzar did come and destroy the city of Jerusalem, Jeremiah was right in the midst of it. Jeremiah is the one speaking in these verses.

> I am the man who has seen affliction by the rod of his wrath. ... Surely he turns his hand against me again and again all day long. ... Remember my affliction and my misery, the wormwood and the bitterness. ... This I recall to my mind; therefore I have hope. It is because of Yahweh's loving kindnesses that we are not consumed, because his compassion doesn't fail. ... For the Lord will not cast off forever. For though he causes grief, yet he will have compassion according to the multitude of his loving kindnesses. For he does not afflict willingly, nor grieve the children of men. ... Why does a living man complain, a man for the punishment of his sins? Let us search and try our ways, and turn again to Yahweh. Let's lift up our heart with our hands to God in the heavens. We have transgressed and have rebelled. You have not pardoned. ... I called on your name, Yahweh, out of the lowest dungeon. You heard my voice: "Don't hide your ear from my sighing, and my cry." You came near in the day that I called on you. You said, "Don't be afraid." (Lamentations 3:1, 3, 19, 21-22, 31-33, 39-42, 55-57)

Jeremiah told us it's because God loves us that we're not utterly consumed by his wrath. Why should we complain about getting in trouble with God when we sin against him? We're supposed to search ourselves and turn to God. One of the reasons God raptured the believers and is sending his wrath is because God hasn't yet pardoned the people sinning against him. They don't have a saving relationship with Jesus. God needs sinners to come to him. Don't you see, this happened because God wants to see your soul saved. How is that not a loving act?

> The Lord is not slow concerning his promise, as some count slowness; but he is patient with us, not wishing that anyone should perish, but that all should come to repentance. (2 Peter 3:9)

Remember that God is both perfectly loving and just. He loves every single person he ever created. He wants what's best for each person. Our earthly selves demand justice when someone wrongs us. We wrong God every single day because we're sinners. He is just when he disciplines and punishes wicked and sinful behavior. See his love for you in this dark storm and be saved.

> God's love has been poured into our hearts through the Holy Spirit who was given to us. ... God commends his own love toward us, in that while we were yet sinners, Christ died for us. Much more then, being now justified by his blood, we will be saved from God's wrath through him. (Romans 5:5, 8-9)

16.2. Why Did God Allow Sin?

Firstly, because we have free will. We were created with the ability to choose to obey God or not. God gave Adam and Eve one rule: don't eat from the Tree of the Knowledge of Good and Evil. Adam chose to disobey God when he ate from that tree. In these verses, "the man" is Adam.

> Yahweh God commanded the man, saying, "You may freely eat of every tree of the garden; but you

shall not eat of the tree of the knowledge of good
and evil; for in the day that you eat of it, you will
surely die." (Genesis 2:16-17)

God isn't the one who tempted or convinced Adam
to eat from the tree. In fact, no one did. He just flat out
chose to. Eve is the one who was tempted, and then
she chose to believe Satan's lies over God's truth and
ate the forbidden fruit. They both made a choice to sin.
James, the half-brother and a disciple of Jesus,
explains temptation in these verses.

> Let no man say when he is tempted, "I am
> tempted by God," for God can't be tempted by evil,
> and he himself tempts no one. But each one is
> tempted when he is drawn away by his own lust
> and enticed. Then the lust, when it has conceived,
> bears sin. The sin, when it is full grown, produces
> death. Don't be deceived, my beloved brothers.
> Every good gift and every perfect gift is from
> above, coming down from the Father of lights,
> with whom can be no variation, nor turning
> shadow. Of his own will he gave birth to us by the
> word of truth, that we should be a kind of first
> fruits of his creatures. (James 1:13-18)

With this free will that we have, we can choose life
or death. If we choose to love God and obey him, we
get life. Moses, "I" in these verses, describes the choice
we have.

> I call heaven and earth to witness against you
> today that I have set before you life and death,
> the blessing and the curse. Therefore choose life,
> that you may live, you and your descendants, to
> love Yahweh your God, to obey his voice, and to
> cling to him; for he is your life. (Deuteronomy
> 30:19-20)

Or if we think it's evil to serve God, we can choose
to follow false gods instead. Joshua is the one
speaking in this verse.

> If it seems evil to you to serve Yahweh, choose today whom you will serve; whether the gods which your fathers served that were beyond the River, or the gods of the Amorites, in whose land you dwell; but as for me and my house, we will serve Yahweh. (Joshua 24:15)

Second, we know that God allows us to be tempted into sinning. He allowed Satan to tempt Eve with the fruit on the Tree of the Knowledge of Good and Evil. God allows this because temptation tests our faith. It produces maturity and trust when we resist it and when we don't sin. God allows sin so that our faith can grow. God allows sin so that we can overcome it and be rewarded in heaven. James explains that to us in these verses.

> The testing of your faith produces endurance. Let endurance have its perfect work, that you may be perfect and complete, lacking in nothing. ... Blessed is a person who endures temptation, for when he has been approved, he will receive the crown of life, which the Lord promised to those who love him. (James 1:3-4, 12)

Lastly, sin allows God to show us exactly how much he loves us. Without sin, Jesus wouldn't have sacrificed his life for you. There would have been no need. God demonstrated his love for you by giving you Jesus. How would you know God loved you otherwise? We've already learned that dying for someone is the ultimate display of love for them. To go along with this, how would God know that you love him if there wasn't any sin? By choosing to believe in Jesus and choosing to overcome sin, you are showing God how much you love him. In these verses, God's "one and only Son" is Jesus.

> For God so loved the world, that he gave his one and only Son, that whoever believes in him should not perish, but have eternal life. For God didn't send his Son into the world to judge the

world, but that the world should be saved through him. (John 3:16-17)

Sin enabled God to display his love, mercy, and his grace. The apostle Paul explains that to us in these verses.

God, being rich in mercy, for his great love with which he loved us, even when we were dead through our trespasses, made us alive together with Christ—by grace you have been saved— and raised us up with him, and made us to sit with him in the heavenly places in Christ Jesus, that in the ages to come he might show the exceeding riches of his grace in kindness toward us in Christ Jesus; for by grace you have been saved through faith, and that not of yourselves; it is the gift of God, not of works, that no one would boast. (Ephesians 2:6-9)

God allows sin because he loves us, and it reveals his love for us. We're his masterpiece after all.

For we are God's masterpiece. He has created us anew in Christ Jesus, so we can do the good things he planned for us long ago. (Ephesians 2:10 NLT)

16.3. Why Did God Create People Who Would End Up In Hell?

Since God knows the beginning and end, many of you may wonder why he created people who would end up in hell. God didn't have to create us to fulfill some need of his. He's perfect in every way. He created us because he wanted to. We bring him great joy. Even though we're sinners and rebel against him, he still loves each of us unconditionally. Remember that he's the very definition of perfect love. He provides an unconditional love without bounds.

God created us in his image, to have dominion over the earth, and to have fellowship with him.

God said, "Let's make man in our image, after
our likeness." ... God created man in his own
image. In God's image he created him; male and
female he created them. God blessed them. God
said to them, "Be fruitful, multiply, fill the earth,
and subdue it. Have dominion over the fish of
the sea, over the birds of the sky, and over every
living thing that moves on the earth." God said,
"Behold, I have given you every herb yielding
seed, which is on the surface of all the earth, and
every tree, which bears fruit yielding seed. It will
be your food. To every animal of the earth, and
to every bird of the sky, and to everything that
creeps on the earth, in which there is life, I have
given every green herb for food;" and it was so.
God saw everything that he had made, and,
behold, it was very good. (Genesis 1:26-31)

God's plan is for us to inherit all things. We'll be
his son or daughter. Jesus's disciple John describes
the inheritance God will give all of his believers in
these verses.

Now I saw a new heaven and a new earth, for the
first heaven and the first earth had passed away.
Also there was no more sea. ... And I heard a loud
voice from heaven saying, "Behold, the
tabernacle of God [is] with men, and He will
dwell with them, and they shall be His people.
God Himself will be with them [and be] their
God. And God will wipe away every tear from
their eyes; there shall be no more death, nor
sorrow, nor crying. There shall be no more pain,
for the former things have passed away. ... He
who overcomes shall inherit all things, and I will
be his God and he shall be My son." (Revelation
21:1, 3-4, 7 NKJV)

Your eternal destination is your choice. We all sin,
and we all need forgiveness of that sin in order to dwell
with God in eternity. That's why God sent Jesus to die
for us. He doesn't want anyone to go to hell. Refer to

2 Peter 3:9 in Chapter 16.1. Remember that he created hell for the fallen angels, not for us. But that's where people who don't want to live with God end up.

> But God commends his own love toward us, in that while we were yet sinners, Christ died for us. (Romans 5:8)

People who've had children know those children aren't going to be perfect. Parents know they messed up as a child and they know their own child will make mistakes and get into trouble as well. Yet, parents choose to have children anyway. Why? Because they want the joy that children bring. Parents teach their children what's right and wrong and hope they will make the right choices when they grow up. It's the same with us and God. We have a choice.

> Train up a child in the way he should go, and when he is old he will not depart from it. (Proverbs 22:6)

King Solomon tells us that children are a reward. They are heirs. This applies to people as well as God. We are God's reward and his heirs. He wants a quiver full of children. Put your faith in Jesus and become an heir to all of God's promises.

> Behold, children are a heritage of Yahweh. The fruit of the womb is his reward. As arrows in the hand of a mighty man, so are the children of youth. Happy is the man who has his quiver full of them. (Psalm 127:3-5)

16.4. Can I Lose My Salvation?

If you've put your faith in Jesus Christ because you know that he died for your sins, then no, you can't lose your salvation. You can't earn your way into heaven. The opposite of that is true as well, you can't be withdrawn from heaven. Your salvation isn't dependent on what you do or don't do. It's a gift from God. When you chose to believe and accepted God's gift, that secured your eternal future once and for all.

It doesn't matter what you've done since you placed your faith in Jesus. Jesus died for all your sins. That includes your future sins too. You are now sealed with the Holy Spirit. In this Scripture, "in him" is a reference to Jesus.

> In him you also, having heard the word of the truth, the Good News of your salvation—in whom, having also believed, you were sealed with the promised Holy Spirit, who is a pledge of our inheritance, to the redemption of God's own possession, to the praise of his glory. (Ephesians 1:13-14)

God's word tells us that nothing can remove you from the hands of God. Not even the power of hell, Satan himself. The apostle Paul tells us that in these verses. "Angels," "principalities," and "powers," all refer to Satan and the other fallen angels who follow him.

> For I am persuaded that neither death, nor life, nor angels, nor principalities, nor things present, nor things to come, nor powers, nor height, nor depth, nor any other created thing will be able to separate us from God's love which is in Christ Jesus our Lord. (Romans 8:38-39)

In these verses, Jesus is the one speaking. He has you, his sheep, securely in his hand. Who could possibly take you out of the hand that is greater and stronger than all other hands? No one.

> My sheep hear my voice, and I know them, and they follow me. I give eternal life to them. They will never perish, and no one will snatch them out of my hand. My Father who has given them to me is greater than all. No one is able to snatch them out of my Father's hand. I and the Father are one. (John 10:27-30)

You can also be confident of your salvation

because God doesn't change his mind. He saved you. He will never leave you or forsake you.

> God is not a man, that he should lie, nor a son of man, that he should repent. Has he said, and he won't do it? Or has he spoken, and he won't make it good? (Numbers 23:19)

God confirmed what he said about your salvation with an oath. God promised to save you from your sins, to send you a savior. God then swore on that promise with his own name since he cannot lie. Then God made good on that promise by sending Jesus to save you. As the apostle Paul says below, this should be an anchor for your soul. You are firm and secure.

> People swear by someone greater than themselves, and the oath confirms what is said and puts an end to all argument. Because God wanted to make the unchanging nature of his purpose very clear to the heirs of what was promised, he confirmed it with an oath. God did this so that, by two unchangeable things in which it is impossible for God to lie, we who have fled to take hold of the hope set before us may be greatly encouraged. We have this hope as an anchor for the soul, firm and secure. It enters the inner sanctuary behind the curtain, where our forerunner, Jesus, has entered on our behalf. (Hebrews 6:16-20 NIV)

16.5. Should I Obey The One World Government?

Yes and no. It depends on what you've been asked to do. God has told us that he puts leaders in their position. That's all leaders, whether you regard them as good or bad. All leaders, every one of them, get their authority from God. So that means even the Antichrist gets his authority from God.

The prophet Daniel told us that God removes kings

and sets up kings.

> Daniel answered, "Blessed be the name of God
> forever and ever; for wisdom and might are his.
> ... He removes kings and sets up kings." (Daniel
> 2:20-21)

Here the apostle Paul tells us about this truth from
God. God is the one who gives someone authority. We
learn that God puts leaders in place for many reasons:
they are servants of God, they are for our good, they
are an avenger of wrath against evil. We're supposed
to obey them so that we don't experience God's wrath
and also for the sake of our own conscience.

> Let every soul be in subjection to the higher
> authorities, for there is no authority except from
> God, and those who exist are ordained by God.
> Therefore he who resists the authority
> withstands the ordinance of God; and those who
> withstand will receive to themselves judgment.
> For rulers are not a terror to the good work, but
> to the evil. Do you desire to have no fear of the
> authority? Do that which is good, and you will
> have praise from the authority, for he is a servant
> of God to you for good. But if you do that which
> is evil, be afraid, for he doesn't bear the sword in
> vain; for he is a servant of God, an avenger for
> wrath to him who does evil. Therefore you need
> to be in subjection, not only because of the
> wrath, but also for conscience' sake. For this
> reason you also pay taxes, for they are servants
> of God's service, continually doing this very
> thing. Therefore give everyone what you owe: if
> you owe taxes, pay taxes; if customs, then
> customs; if respect, then respect; if honor, then
> honor. (Romans 13:1-7)

We're supposed to honor and respect higher
authorities because God is the one behind the scenes
directing what they're doing. You should submit to
government leaders, leaders in your workplace,

leaders at school, and any other kind of leader. When you submit to them, you're submitting to God. Don't make their job harder by being disobedient.

> Obey your leaders and submit to them, for they watch on behalf of your souls, as those who will give account, that they may do this with joy, and not with groaning, for that would be unprofitable for you. (Hebrews 13:17)

Since leaders are sinful people too, that means there will be times they choose to rebel against God and ask you to do the same. This is when you need to disobey them. You need to obey God above anyone else. In these verses, we see Peter and the apostles explain this. "This man's blood" is a reference to Jesus's crucifixion.

> The high priest questioned them, saying, "Didn't we strictly command you not to teach in this name? Behold, you have filled Jerusalem with your teaching, and intend to bring this man's blood on us." But Peter and the apostles answered, "We must obey God rather than men." (Acts 5:27-29)

Now I know I've confused you because I said God is directing their steps, yet some rebel against God. So how does that work? Even when the leaders rebel against him, God uses that for our good. That's one of the ways God disciplines us, with bad leaders. Remember that Israel was taken into captivity several times. They were subjected to terrible leaders who enslaved them. God was in control of that. He sent those leaders to overthrow the Israelite cities because the people had turned away from him and sinned. Those evil rulers got the Israelites to remember God, realize they sinned, and reach out to him for help. After the people turned back to God, the evil ruler got punished by God.

This is how it works with the Antichrist too. He is

an evil ruler possessed by Satan. So he's rebelling against God. The wrath he unleashes will turn many people toward God. The wrath will also punish the wicked people who never intend to put their faith in Jesus, the people who don't want anything to do with God. In the end, when the tribulation period is over, God will deal with the Antichrist and Satan. Until then, he will use them to accomplish his will.

There will be times you shouldn't obey the Antichrist or his government or even other leaders in your life. If they ask you to support or partake in something you know is against God's word, don't do it. Don't take the mark of the Antichrist for example. You know that God's word says not to, that it'll seal your eternal fate because you'll be choosing Satan over God. So don't do that. Will the cost of obedience to God be high? Most certainly. You already know that though. The Antichrist will kill many people who put their faith in Jesus. Remember that Jesus was obedient to God through his own death. If he's living inside you, he will help you do the same.

Daniel, the Old Testament prophet, was a great example of obeying God over all else. Let's see what happened to Daniel. In these verses, "Darius" is the king of Babylon.

> It pleased Darius to set over the kingdom one hundred twenty local governors ... and over them three presidents, of whom Daniel was one.... Then this Daniel was distinguished above the presidents and the local governors, because an excellent spirit was in him; and the king thought to set him over the whole realm. Then the presidents and the local governors sought to find occasion against Daniel as touching the kingdom; but they could find no occasion or fault, because he was faithful. There wasn't any error or fault found in him. Then these men said, "We won't find any occasion against this Daniel, unless we find it against him concerning the law of his God." ... All the presidents of the kingdom, the deputies and the local governors, the

counselors and the governors, have consulted
together to establish a royal statute, and to make
a strong decree, that whoever asks a petition of
any god or man for thirty days, except of you, O
king, he shall be cast into the den of lions. ...
Therefore king Darius signed the writing and the
decree. When Daniel knew that the writing was
signed, he went into his house (now his windows
were open in his room toward Jerusalem) and he
kneeled on his knees three times a day, and
prayed, and gave thanks before his God, as he
did before. ... Then they answered and said
before the king, "That Daniel, who is of the
children of the captivity of Judah, doesn't
respect you, O king, nor the decree that you have
signed, but makes his petition three times a day."
... Then the king commanded, and they brought
Daniel, and cast him into the den of lions. The
king spoke and said to Daniel, "Your God whom
you serve continually, he will deliver you." ...
Then the king arose very early in the morning,
and went in haste to the den of lions. When he
came near to the den to Daniel, he cried with a
troubled voice. The king spoke and said to
Daniel, "Daniel, servant of the living God, is your
God, whom you serve continually, able to deliver
you from the lions?" Then Daniel said to the
king, "O king, live forever! My God has sent his
angel, and has shut the lions' mouths, and they
have not hurt me; because as before him
innocence was found in me; and also before you,
O king, I have done no harm." Then the king was
exceedingly glad, and commanded that they
should take Daniel up out of the den. So Daniel
was taken up out of the den, and no kind of harm
was found on him, because he had trusted in his
God. (Daniel 6:2-4, 7, 9-10, 13, 16, 19-23)

A law was enacted that told people they could only
worship the king. Daniel refused to worship the king.
He worshiped God just like he always had done. He
also did it so everyone could see him do it, with the

windows open. The punishment for not worshiping the king was death by lion. Since Daniel was obedient to God and had such great faith, we learn that God saved him from that ordeal by shutting the lions' mouths. Notice that God didn't remove Daniel from the ordeal, instead he was with him through it. Daniel was able to display his faith for all to see.

It may well be that God intends to do something just as miraculous for you for being obedient to him and having strong faith.

16.6. How Do I Protect Myself From Evil

Paul the apostle gave us a really great visual and tool for protecting our self against evil. It's called the "armor of God." He says we need to be protected with armor and have a sword. But this is no ordinary armor of chain mail with a sword of steel. This armor protects against evil and the sword of the Spirit reveals truth.

> Put on the whole armor of God, that you may be able to stand against the wiles of the devil. For our wrestling is not against flesh and blood, but against the principalities, against the powers, against the world's rulers of the darkness of this age, and against the spiritual forces of wickedness in the heavenly places. Therefore put on the whole armor of God, that you may be able to withstand in the evil day, and having done all, to stand. Stand therefore, having the utility belt of truth buckled around your waist, and having put on the breastplate of righteousness, and having fitted your feet with the preparation of the Good News of peace, above all, taking up the shield of faith, with which you will be able to quench all the fiery darts of the evil one. And take the helmet of salvation, and the sword of the Spirit, which is the word of God; with all prayer and requests, praying at all times in the Spirit, and being watchful to this end in all perseverance and requests for all the saints:

on my behalf, that utterance may be given to me in opening my mouth, to make known with boldness the mystery of the Good News, for which I am an ambassador in chains; that in it I may speak boldly, as I ought to speak. (Ephesians 6:11-20)

The first thing Paul tells us after mentioning this armor is that we have to know who the enemy is. The enemy isn't "flesh and blood." That means it's not people. The enemy is Satan and his "spiritual forces of wickedness." You can't fight Satan with human means. You need godly protection and a godly weapon in this spiritual war.

Let's look at the elements in this armor. The "belt of truth" is God's word. You need to know your Bible. Have it stored in your heart and close to you, ready to use like a tool you'd pull out of a utility belt. The "breastplate of righteousness" is you placing your faith in Jesus. He's the one who makes you righteous. Having "fitted your feet" with the gospel means you're able to demonstrate your faith in both words and actions. The "shield of faith" is you knowing and calling on all the promises of God when Satan's attack comes against you. Do not be afraid. Have hope. Your "helmet of salvation" is being fully confident that you have been saved through your faith in Jesus. You are sealed with the Holy Spirit.

The "sword of the Spirit" is your weapon. It's the Word of God. When Satan came against Jesus to tempt him in the wilderness, Jesus combated Satan's lies with Scripture. There is power in the Word of God. Use it.

For the word of God is living and active, and sharper than any two-edged sword, piercing even to the dividing of soul and spirit, of both joints and marrow, and is able to discern the thoughts and intentions of the heart. (Hebrews 4:12)

After you've put on your armor, you need to pray at all times. You need to be close to God in order to draw strength from him. You get close to God by talking to God and reading his word.

> Always rejoice. Pray without ceasing. In everything give thanks, for this is the will of God in Christ Jesus toward you. (1 Thessalonians 5:16-18)

> He who dwells in the secret place of the Most High will rest in the shadow of the Almighty. I will say of Yahweh, "He is my refuge and my fortress; my God, in whom I trust." For he will deliver you from the snare of the fowler, and from the deadly pestilence. He will cover you with his feathers. Under his wings you will take refuge. His faithfulness is your shield and rampart. ... Because you have made Yahweh your refuge, and the Most High your dwelling place, no evil shall happen to you, neither shall any plague come near your dwelling. For he will put his angels in charge of you, to guard you in all your ways. (Psalm 91:1-4, 9-11)

Now you're ready to stand firm when evil comes against you.

> It is God who enables us, along with you, to stand firm for Christ. He has commissioned us, and he has identified us as his own by placing the Holy Spirit in our hearts as the first installment that guarantees everything he has promised us. (2 Corinthians 1:21-22)

Part 7
What's Next?

Chapter 17 - I'm A Believer, What's Next For Me?

As someone left behind in the wake of the rapture, I'm sure you're wondering what happens now? What should you expect in the coming years? How can you be prepared?

First things first. If you've come to know who Jesus Christ is and you believe he died for your sins, then you have absolutely nothing to worry about. Your soul is saved. You can be 100 percent sure of that. These Scriptures, written by Paul the apostle, reiterate this truth.

> Now I declare to you, brothers, the Good News which I preached to you, which also you received, in which you also stand, by which also you are saved, if you hold firmly the word which I preached to you—unless you believed in vain. For I delivered to you first of all that which I also received: that Christ died for our sins according to the Scriptures, that he was buried, that he was raised on the third day according to the Scriptures. (1 Corinthians 15:1-4)

> If you will confess with your mouth that Jesus is Lord, and believe in your heart that God raised him from the dead, you will be saved. ... For, "Whoever will call on the name of the Lord will be saved." (Romans 10:9, 13)

As a believer, one of two things will happen to you. Either you will live through the tribulation events or you will die as a tribulation saint. There is not another rapture that's going to happen.

17.1. If You Live Through The Tribulation

The tribulation events last seven years, and the Bible tells us that very few people will live through the horrors. If you are one of the lucky ones who survive, then you can look forward to seeing Jesus at his second coming. He will physically return to earth on the Mount of Olives in Israel at the end of the seven year period. He will reign physically on earth for 1,000 years. You'll be included in Jesus's kingdom on earth.

This is what you'll see at the end of the tribulation period. Heaven will open and Jesus will come out riding a white horse. He'll have crowns on his head and a robe sprinkled with blood. He will come against the Antichrist, who is the "beast," and his armies who have gathered.

> I saw the heaven opened, and behold, a white horse, and he who sat on it is called Faithful and True. In righteousness he judges and makes war. His eyes are a flame of fire, and on his head are many crowns. He has names written and a name written which no one knows but he himself. He is clothed in a garment sprinkled with blood. His name is called "The Word of God." ... He has on his garment and on his thigh a name written, "KING OF KINGS, AND LORD OF LORDS." ... I saw the beast, and the kings of the earth, and their armies, gathered together to make war against him who sat on the horse, and against his army. (Revelation 19:11-13, 16, 19)

Then Jesus, "the Son of Man," will separate those who are still alive. The believers, the "sheep," will be separated from the unbelievers, the "goats." Only the believers get to live with him in his kingdom.

> But when the Son of Man comes in his glory, and all the holy angels with him, then he will sit on the throne of his glory. Before him all the nations

will be gathered, and he will separate them one from another, as a shepherd separates the sheep from the goats. He will set the sheep on his right hand, but the goats on the left. Then the King will tell those on his right hand, "Come, blessed of my Father, inherit the Kingdom prepared for you from the foundation of the world." (Matthew 25:31-34)

As a believer, you'll hear Jesus say, "Come, blessed of my Father, inherit the Kingdom prepared for you from the foundation of the world."

17.2. If You Die As A Tribulation Saint

If you die during the tribulation period, it's likely because you'll be martyred for your faith in Jesus. However, there's a great reward waiting for you in heaven. As a tribulation saint you have the privilege of worshiping at the feet of Jesus. This reminds me of an encounter Jesus had with Mary and Martha during his ministry on earth. Jesus was in their house speaking with a group of people. Mary was sitting at Jesus's feet, listening attentively (Luke 10:39). I'm sure she was in awe. You'll be in awe as well. In this Scripture, the "great suffering" is the tribulation period.

After these things I looked, and behold, a great multitude, which no man could count, out of every nation and of all tribes, peoples, and languages, standing before the throne and before the Lamb, dressed in white robes, with palm branches in their hands. They cried with a loud voice, saying, "Salvation be to our God, who sits on the throne, and to the Lamb!" All the angels were standing around the throne, the elders, and the four living creatures; and they fell on their faces before his throne, and worshiped God, saying, "Amen! Blessing, glory, wisdom, thanksgiving, honor, power, and might, be to our God forever and ever! Amen." One of the elders answered, saying to me, "These who are arrayed

> in the white robes, who are they, and where did they come from?" I told him, "My lord, you know." He said to me, "These are those who came out of the great suffering. They washed their robes, and made them white in the Lamb's blood. Therefore they are before the throne of God, they serve him day and night in his temple. He who sits on the throne will spread his tabernacle over them. They will never be hungry or thirsty any more. The sun won't beat on them, nor any heat; for the Lamb who is in the middle of the throne shepherds them and leads them to springs of life-giving waters. And God will wipe away every tear from their eyes." (Revelation 7:9-17)

You'll never be thirsty, hungry, or scorched by the sun again. Jesus, the "Lamb," will take care of you. God will wipe away every one of your tears.

You'll also be at the second coming of Jesus, but you'll have a heavenly point of view of that event. You'll be in the army following Jesus on white horses and dressed in fine linen. In this Scripture, Jesus is the one called "Faithful and True."

> I saw the heaven opened, and behold, a white horse, and he who sat on it is called Faithful and True. In righteousness he judges and makes war. ... The armies which are in heaven, clothed in white, pure, fine linen, followed him on white horses. (Revelation 19:11, 14)

Then after Jesus returns to earth, that's when you get your resurrected, eternal, glorious body! After you've been resurrected, you'll reign with Jesus on earth for the next 1,000 years.

> And I saw the souls of those who had been beheaded for their testimony about Jesus and for proclaiming the word of God. They had not worshiped the beast or his statue, nor accepted

his mark on their forehead or their hands. They all came to life again, and they reigned with Christ for a thousand years. This is the first resurrection. (The rest of the dead did not come back to life until the thousand years had ended.) Blessed and holy are those who share in the first resurrection. For them the second death holds no power, but they will be priests of God and of Christ and will reign with him a thousand years. (Revelation 20:4-6 NLT)

Don't be afraid. As a believer, there are wonderful things that await you in heaven. These verses tell us those things include a new body, eternal life, and citizenship in heaven.

For our citizenship is in heaven, from where we also wait for a Savior, the Lord Jesus Christ, who will change the body of our humiliation to be conformed to the body of his glory, according to the working by which he is able even to subject all things to himself. (Philippians 3:20-21)

One who believes in the Son has eternal life. (John 3:36)

Chapter 18 - I Don't Believe, What's Next For Me?

If you have hardened your heart against God and don't believe he loves you and you don't believe that he sent Jesus to die for your sins, then nothing good awaits you. There's no sugar coating this. You will meet Jesus, but he'll be your judge instead of your savior. Your destination is not heaven but hell, the lake of fire God created for the wicked, fallen angels. It's not the party place that Hollywood makes it out to be.

Because your heart is hard, these verses indicate that you are storing up wrath for yourself.

> According to your hardness and unrepentant heart you are treasuring up for yourself wrath in the day of wrath ... God; who "will pay back to everyone according to their works:" ... to those who are self-seeking, and don't obey the truth, but obey unrighteousness, will be wrath, indignation, oppression, and anguish on every soul of man who does evil. (Romans 2:5-6, 8-9)

> Blessed is the man who always fears; but one who hardens his heart falls into trouble. (Proverbs 28:14)

> One who believes in the Son has eternal life, but one who disobeys the Son won't see life, but the wrath of God remains on him. (John 3:36)

You will have to give an account of your life to God. You won't have anyone to come to your defense. Instead, you'll just have the worst of accusers against you, Satan. Remember that he's been accusing you day and night before God. Your name won't be "written in the Book of Life" which is Jesus's book, because you didn't place your faith in Jesus. In these verses, God is the "judge of the living and the dead."

They will give account to him who is ready to judge the living and the dead. (1 Peter 4:5)

I saw the dead, the great and the small, standing before the throne, and they opened books. Another book was opened, which is the book of life. The dead were judged out of the things which were written in the books, according to their works. The sea gave up the dead who were in it. Death and Hades gave up the dead who were in them. They were judged, each one according to his works. Death and Hades were thrown into the lake of fire. This is the second death, the lake of fire. If anyone was not found written in the book of life, he was cast into the lake of fire. (Revelation 20:12-15)

What if you're one of the lucky ones who survive the tribulation period on earth? Does that count as time served and now you get to go free? No. Even if you survive the tribulation as a sinner who hasn't been forgiven, your destiny is still hell. The Bible tells us that when Jesus returns at his second coming that one of the things he does is put all the unbelievers in the lake of fire.

This Scripture shows Jesus, the "Son of Man," at his second coming. He separates the "sheep," who are the believers, and the "goats," who are the unbelievers. All the goats are put in the lake of fire.

But when the Son of Man comes in his glory, and all the holy angels with him, then he will sit on the throne of his glory. Before him all the nations will be gathered, and he will separate them one from another, as a shepherd separates the sheep from the goats. He will set the sheep on his right hand, but the goats on the left. ... Then he will say also to those on the left hand, "Depart from me, you cursed, into the eternal fire which is prepared for the devil and his angels." (Matthew 25:31-33, 41)

These verses are a parable, a story with a moral,

that Jesus told. He even explained what the story meant to his disciples afterwards. The "children of the evil one," Satan, are gathered up and burned with fire. If you haven't put your faith in Jesus, the "Son of Man," then by default you're a child of Satan. This parable portrays what happens when Jesus is harvesting the earth at his second coming.

> He set another parable before them, saying, "The Kingdom of Heaven is like a man who sowed good seed in his field, but while people slept, his enemy came and sowed darnel weeds also among the wheat, and went away. But when the blade sprang up and produced grain, then the darnel weeds appeared also. ... 'Let both grow together until the harvest, and in the harvest time I will tell the reapers, "First, gather up the darnel weeds, and bind them in bundles to burn them; but gather the wheat into my barn." ' " ... Then Jesus sent the multitudes away, and went into the house. His disciples came to him, saying, "Explain to us the parable of the darnel weeds of the field." He answered them, "He who sows the good seed is the Son of Man, the field is the world, the good seeds are the children of the Kingdom, and the darnel weeds are the children of the evil one. The enemy who sowed them is the devil. The harvest is the end of the age, and the reapers are angels. As therefore the darnel weeds are gathered up and burned with fire; so will it be at the end of this age. The Son of Man will send out his angels, and they will gather out of his Kingdom all things that cause stumbling and those who do iniquity, and will cast them into the furnace of fire. There will be weeping and gnashing of teeth." (Matthew 13:24-26, 30, 36-42)

I can't imagine how impossibly difficult it will be to survive the tribulation events. Don't let your perseverance go to waste by spending eternity in hell. Make a better choice.

As God's Holy Spirit says in these verses, "don't harden your hearts" in rebellion today. Answer God's call instead.

> Therefore, even as the Holy Spirit says, "Today if you will hear his voice, don't harden your hearts, as in the rebellion, in the day of the trial in the wilderness, where your fathers tested me and tried me, and saw my deeds for forty years. Therefore I was displeased with that generation, and said, 'They always err in their heart, but they didn't know my ways.' As I swore in my wrath, 'They will not enter into my rest.' " Beware, brothers, lest perhaps there might be in any one of you an evil heart of unbelief, in falling away from the living God; but exhort one another day by day, so long as it is called "today", lest any one of you be hardened by the deceitfulness of sin. For we have become partakers of Christ, if we hold the beginning of our confidence firm to the end. (Hebrews 3:7-14)

In this Scripture, we learn there's a choice set before us by God. A choice between life and death. Let Jesus love you by accepting what he did to save you from your sins. Choose life.

> Behold, I have set before you today life and prosperity, and death and evil. For I command you today to love Yahweh your God, to walk in his ways and to keep his commandments, his statutes, and his ordinances, that you may live and multiply, and that Yahweh your God may bless you .... But if your heart turns away, and you will not hear, but are drawn away and worship other gods, and serve them, I declare to you today that you will surely perish. You will not prolong your days .... I call heaven and earth to witness against you today that I have set before you life and death, the blessing and the curse. Therefore choose life, that you may live. (Deuteronomy 30:15-19)

Chapter 19 - Timeline Of Events

There are many events the Bible describes that take place after the rapture, during the tribulation period, and after the second coming of Jesus. We'll take a look at some key events so that you can be prepared for what lies ahead.

19.1. The Antichrist Becomes A Global Leader

After the rapture, the first thing you should be looking for is the rise of a global leader. The Bible refers to this person as the Antichrist because he will be the opposite of and opposed to Christ and all things godly. This person will come on the scene as a political leader with the ability to unite all the people on the earth. One of the ways he'll be able to do that is with religion. He will also be seen as a religious leader who brings all the faiths together. He will be a master of finance and economics and have solutions to the troubles that are plaguing the planet as a result of the rapture. His primary message will be one of peace and security. As I mentioned in Part 4 of this book, he will be well liked, and you'll desire to listen to and follow him.

This verse tells us the Antichrist, "the ruler," will be a political leader and make a treaty with God's people, Israel, for seven years.

> The ruler will make a treaty with the people for a period of one set of seven, but after half this time, he will put an end to the sacrifices and offerings. And as a climax to all his terrible deeds, he will set up a sacrilegious object that causes desecration, until the fate decreed for this defiler is finally poured out on him. (Daniel 9:27 NLT)

The Antichrist, who is the "first beast" in this Scripture, will be a religious leader. The False Prophet, who is "another beast," will cause everyone on earth to worship the Antichrist.

> I saw another beast coming up out of the earth. He had two horns like a lamb, and he spoke like a dragon. He exercises all the authority of the first beast in his presence. He makes the earth and those who dwell in it to worship the first beast, whose fatal wound was healed. (Revelation 13:11-12)

The Antichrist, "he" and "beast" in these verses, will be an economic leader because everyone must have his mark in order to buy or sell.

> He causes all, the small and the great, the rich and the poor, and the free and the slave, to be given marks on their right hands, or on their foreheads; and that no one would be able to buy or to sell, unless he has that mark, which is the name of the beast or the number of his name. (Revelation 13:16-17)

The rapture of Jesus's followers is what enabled the Antichrist to rise. The restrainer who was holding him back is the Holy Spirit. The Holy Spirit resided in each person who believed in Jesus Christ. Even though the Holy Spirit was removed, he is still at work in the world convicting people of their sin so that they will come to know God.

In these verses, the "man of sin," "son of destruction," and "lawless one" all refer to the Antichrist.

> Now, brothers, concerning the coming of our Lord Jesus Christ and our gathering together to him.... ... Let no one deceive you in any way. For it will not be, unless the rebellion comes first, and the man of sin is revealed, the son of destruction, he who opposes and exalts himself against all that is called God or that is worshiped, so that he sits as God in the temple of God, setting himself up as God. ... Now you know what is restraining him, to the end that he may be revealed in his own season. For the mystery of

lawlessness already works. Only there is one who restrains now, until he is taken out of the way. Then the lawless one will be revealed, whom the Lord will kill with the breath of his mouth, and destroy by the manifestation of his coming; even he whose coming is according to the working of Satan with all power and signs and lying wonders. (2 Thessalonians 2:1, 3-4, 6-9)

This Scripture tells us why the Holy Spirit had to be removed before the Antichrist, "the enemy," could rise as a leader. Because the believers filled with that Holy Spirit would have risen up against him.

When the enemy comes in like a flood, The Spirit of the LORD will lift up a standard against him. (Isaiah 59:19 NKJV)

In these verses, spoken by Jesus, we see the Holy Spirit, who is the "Counselor" and "Spirit of truth," is still at work in the world. He's convicting people of their sin so that they'll turn to Jesus for salvation.

Nevertheless I tell you the truth: It is to your advantage that I go away, for if I don't go away, the Counselor won't come to you. But if I go, I will send him to you. When he has come, he will convict the world about sin, about righteousness, and about judgment; about sin, because they don't believe in me; about righteousness, because I am going to my Father, and you won't see me any more; about judgment, because the prince of this world has been judged. ... However when he, the Spirit of truth, has come, he will guide you into all truth, for he will not speak from himself; but whatever he hears, he will speak. He will declare to you things that are coming. (John 16:7-11, 13)

Once this global leader, "the ruler," brings order back to the planet, he will work to achieve what no other person on earth has ever achieved. He will broker a peace deal between Israel and her neighboring enemy countries. In this verse, Israel is referred to as "the people." This peace treaty will be a seven year treaty which is "one set of seven." The signing of this treaty is the event that starts the clock ticking on the tribulation period. The rapture didn't start the actual tribulation period. This peace treaty is what kicks it off.

> The ruler will make a treaty with the people for a period of one set of seven, but after half this time, he will put an end to the sacrifices and offerings. And as a climax to all his terrible deeds, he will set up a sacrilegious object that causes desecration, until the fate decreed for this defiler is finally poured out on him. (Daniel 9:27 NLT)

From this time forward there will be great suffering and anguish on the planet.

> For there will be greater anguish in those days than at any time since God created the world. And it will never be so great again. (Mark 13:19 NLT)

The Bible tells us Israel signs the treaty to gain security or "refuge." I expect Israel's enemies will have increased their attacks against the country or are threatening a massive invasion. Israel, "death," and "Sheol," which is hell, sign the treaty. We learn that Israel, "this people in Jerusalem," knows the treaty is based on lies, yet they sign it anyway.

> Therefore hear Yahweh's word, you scoffers, that rule this people in Jerusalem: "Because you have said, 'We have made a covenant with death, and we are in agreement with Sheol. When the overflowing scourge passes through, it won't come to us; for we have made lies our refuge, and we have hidden ourselves under falsehood.' " Therefore the Lord Yahweh says, "Behold, I lay in Zion for a foundation a stone, a tried stone, a precious cornerstone of a sure foundation. He

who believes shall not act hastily. I will make justice the measuring line, and righteousness the plumb line. The hail will sweep away the refuge of lies, and the waters will overflow the hiding place. Your covenant with death shall be annulled, and your agreement with Sheol shall not stand. When the overflowing scourge passes through, then you will be trampled down by it." (Isaiah 28:14-18)

God will annul the treaty when he returns. This treaty ignites God's anger because the Antichrist breaks up God's holy land with this treaty. In this verse, "I" refers to God, and "my land" refers to Israel.

I will gather all nations, and will bring them down into the valley of Jehoshaphat; and I will execute judgment on them there for my people, and for my heritage, Israel, whom they have scattered among the nations. They have divided my land. (Joel 3:2)

God promised specific land to his chosen people, the Israelites. This Scripture tells us that land spans from the Nile River to the Euphrates River (see also Numbers 34). That land includes the city of Jerusalem.

In that day Yahweh made a covenant with Abram, saying, "I have given this land to your offspring, from the river of Egypt to the great river, the river Euphrates." (Genesis 15:18)

It's a very special city to God because it's the city where Jesus himself will reign on the earth. God will dwell in Jerusalem. God even makes a New Jerusalem when he creates the new heaven and new earth. In these verses, "Zion" refers to Jerusalem.

Again the word of the LORD of hosts came, saying, "Thus says the LORD of hosts: 'I am zealous for Zion with great zeal; With great fervor I am zealous for her.' Thus says the LORD:

'I will return to Zion, And dwell in the midst of Jerusalem. Jerusalem shall be called the City of Truth, The Mountain of the LORD of hosts, The Holy Mountain.'" (Zechariah 8:1-3 NKJV)

I saw a new heaven and a new earth: for the first heaven and the first earth have passed away, and the sea is no more. I saw the holy city, New Jerusalem, coming down out of heaven from God, prepared like a bride adorned for her husband. I heard a loud voice out of heaven saying, "Behold, God's dwelling is with people, and he will dwell with them, and they will be his people, and God himself will be with them as their God." (Revelation 21:1-3)

It shall happen in the latter days, that the mountain of Yahweh's house shall be established on the top of the mountains, and shall be raised above the hills; and all nations shall flow to it. Many peoples shall go and say, "Come, let's go up to the mountain of Yahweh, to the house of the God of Jacob; and he will teach us of his ways, and we will walk in his paths." For the law shall go out of Zion, and Yahweh's word from Jerusalem. He will judge between the nations, and will decide concerning many peoples. They shall beat their swords into plowshares, and their spears into pruning hooks. Nation shall not lift up sword against nation, neither shall they learn war any more. (Isaiah 2:2-4)

Remember that I told you the Antichrist is indwelt by Satan. Satan hates God and wants to destroy God's plans. By breaking up God's land, Satan is shaking his fist at God and rebelling against God's plan.

Don't fret about the treaty and the ire Satan has sparked. God's will shall be done. God always keeps his promises. Jesus already defeated Satan when he died on that cross and conquered death. Satan's time on earth has an expiration date, and he knows it. These verses tell us Satan's time ends after Jesus's

1,000-year reign on earth. Satan is "the devil who deceived" and "the beast" is the Antichrist.

> And after the thousand years, Satan will be released from his prison, and he will come out to deceive the nations which are in the four corners of the earth, Gog and Magog, to gather them together to the war; the number of whom is as the sand of the sea. They went up over the width of the earth, and surrounded the camp of the saints, and the beloved city. Fire came down out of heaven from God and devoured them. The devil who deceived them was thrown into the lake of fire and sulfur, where the beast and the false prophet are also. They will be tormented day and night forever and ever. (Revelation 20:7-10)

19.2. The Tribulation Begins

Let's talk more about this peace treaty and the length of the tribulation period. The tribulation starts sometime after the rapture and ends at the second coming of Jesus. It specifically starts with the signing of the peace treaty between Israel and her enemies.

The Old Testament prophet, Daniel, wrote about the Antichrist and the peace treaty around 539 BC when Babylon was conquered by the Medes. Daniel was praying to God and asking him to forgive the people of Israel of their sins and to turn his anger away from Jerusalem when the angel Gabriel suddenly appeared to answer the questions he was asking God.

Gabriel said the ruler to come, the Antichrist, would make a peace treaty for "one week." The original Hebrew word used for *week* means a period of seven years, so the peace treaty is for seven years. We also see in this Scripture that it says to the "full end" wrath will be poured out. The time of tribulation will last the entire seven years. During this time God will display his wrath with all manner of signs and wonders. It's meant to turn people away from wickedness and toward God. It's God's final warning that time is running out for you to make a choice on where you want to spend eternity.

> He will make a firm covenant with many for one week. In the middle of the week he will cause the sacrifice and the offering to cease. On the wing of abominations will come one who makes desolate; and even to the full end, and that determined, wrath will be poured out on the desolate. (Daniel 9:27)

Jesus spoke of the Tribulation period as well. We see in these verses that he even referenced, thereby validating, the prophecy given by Daniel.

> As he sat on the Mount of Olives, the disciples came to him privately, saying, "Tell us, when will these things be? What is the sign of your coming, and of the end of the age?" ... "When, therefore, you see the abomination of desolation, which was spoken of through Daniel the prophet, standing in the holy place (let the reader understand), then let those who are in Judea flee to the mountains. ... For then there will be great suffering, such as has not been from the beginning of the world until now, no, nor ever will be. Unless those days had been shortened, no flesh would have been saved. But for the sake of the chosen ones, those days will be shortened." (Matthew 24:3, 15-16, 21-22)

We learned above that in the "middle of the week" the Antichrist causes the sacrifices in the Jewish temple to cease because of an abomination he's committed in the temple. The "middle of the week" is three and a half years. The "abomination of desolation" is that he declares himself God and sets up some sacrilegious object in God's temple. He ruins and profanes the temple.

The day of the Lord, "Yahweh," and the great tribulation are other references to this period of time. They also specifically refer to the last three and a half years of the tribulation which will feature very intense wrath from God. During the last three and a half years, God says in these verses that people become "more rare than fine gold."

> Behold, the day of Yahweh comes, cruel, with wrath and fierce anger; to make the land a desolation, and to destroy its sinners out of it. ... I will punish the world for their evil, and the wicked for their iniquity. I will cause the arrogance of the proud to cease, and will humble the arrogance of the terrible. I will make people more rare than fine gold, even a person than the pure gold of Ophir. (Isaiah 13:9, 11-12)

The last three and a half years will feature wonders in the heavens and on earth including blood, fire, and pillars of smoke. In these verses, "Zion" refers to Jerusalem. I hope you choose to see God and his glory in the midst of these signs and that you "tear your heart" and turn to God because he will forgive you.

> Blow the trumpet in Zion, and sound an alarm in my holy mountain! Let all the inhabitants of the land tremble, for the day of Yahweh comes, for it is close at hand: A day of darkness and gloominess, a day of clouds and thick darkness. As the dawn spreading on the mountains, a great and strong people; there has never been the like, neither will there be any more after them, even to the years of many generations. ... Yahweh thunders his voice before his army; for his forces are very great; for he is strong who obeys his command; for the day of Yahweh is great and very awesome, and who can endure it? "Yet even now," says Yahweh, "turn to me with all your heart, and with fasting, and with weeping, and with mourning." Tear your heart, and not your garments, and turn to Yahweh, your God; for he is gracious and merciful, slow to anger, and abundant in loving kindness, and relents from sending calamity. ... I will show wonders in the heavens and in the earth: blood, fire, and pillars

of smoke. The sun will be turned into darkness, and the moon into blood, before the great and terrible day of Yahweh comes. It will happen that whoever will call on Yahweh's name shall be saved; for in Mount Zion and in Jerusalem there will be those who escape, as Yahweh has said, and among the remnant, those whom Yahweh calls. (Joel 2:1-2, 11-13, 30-32)

Jesus expected the people to know of his first coming, so be looking for Jesus and know the day he will return again. In these verses, Jesus is "he" and the city he wept over is Jerusalem. Jesus tells us the people didn't know the "time of your visitation." That means they didn't recognize Jesus visiting them.

When he came near, he saw the city and wept over it, saying, "If you, even you, had known today the things which belong to your peace! But now, they are hidden from your eyes. For the days will come on you, when your enemies will throw up a barricade against you, surround you, hem you in on every side, and will dash you and your children within you to the ground. They will not leave in you one stone on another, because you didn't know the time of your visitation." (Luke 19:41-44)

Once that treaty is signed, you'll be able to figure out to the exact day when Jesus Christ will appear on earth for his second coming. This should give you great hope and eager anticipation for that day. Jesus will return to earth three and a half years after the temple sacrifices are stopped. Since the Jewish calendar uses 360 days per year, it'll be 1,260 days.

This Scripture below mentions 1,290 days. This is because Jesus returns when the war of Armageddon is taking place. It'll take some time to stop that war and then separate out all the unbelievers from those who are still alive. For those who are blessed and survive to the 1,335th day, that's when Jesus's reign on earth begins and believers join him in his kingdom.

> From the time that the continual burnt offering
> is taken away, and the abomination that makes
> desolate set up, there will be one thousand two
> hundred ninety days. Blessed is he who waits,
> and comes to the one thousand three hundred
> thirty-five days. (Daniel 12:11-12)

Everyone will see Jesus, the "Son of Man," coming
on the clouds, but not everyone will be happy to see
him. We see in the Scripture below that many people
will mourn his return. When you see him, I hope you
are only mourning because you have a repentant heart
and recognize what Jesus did for you. In that case,
your sorrow will quickly be replaced by joy.

> Later, Jesus sat on the Mount of Olives. His
> disciples came to him privately and said, "Tell
> us, when will all this happen? What sign will
> signal your return and the end of the world?" ...
> "The day is coming when you will see what
> Daniel   the   prophet   spoke   about—the
> sacrilegious object that causes desecration
> standing in the Holy Place." (Reader, pay
> attention!) ... "Immediately after the anguish of
> those days, the sun will be darkened, the moon
> will give no light, the stars will fall from the sky,
> and the powers in the heavens will be shaken.
> And then at last, the sign that the Son of Man is
> coming will appear in the heavens, and there will
> be deep mourning among all the peoples of the
> earth. And they will see the Son of Man coming
> on the clouds of heaven with power and great
> glory." (Matthew 24:3, 15, 29-30 NLT)

19.3. God Sends Judgments

Once the tribulation period starts, God will send
many judgments to the earth. If you're familiar with
the plagues that God sent against Egypt when Pharaoh
wouldn't let the Israelites go, these judgments are
similar, but far more impactful and devastating. The
terrible things to come include war, famine, poverty,

large hail, widespread fire, scorching heat, water sources turned to blood, boils on people's skin, and lots of death. Death and destruction are the hallmark of these judgments. The Bible tells us millions of people will perish.

The book of Revelation in the Bible depicts the judgments after the rapture. In this verse, we see hail and fire after the first trumpet is sounded. One-third of the earth burns as a result.

> The first sounded, and there followed hail and fire, mixed with blood, and they were thrown to the earth. One third of the earth was burned up, and one third of the trees were burned up, and all green grass was burned up. (Revelation 8:7)

In this verse, we see everything in the sea dies because it's turned to blood.

> The second angel poured out his bowl into the sea, and it became blood as of a dead man. Every living thing in the sea died. (Revelation 16:3)

This Scripture reveals there's severe hail weighing one talent, which is equivalent to 75 pounds.

> Great hailstones, about the weight of a talent, came down out of the sky on people. People blasphemed God because of the plague of the hail, for this plague is exceedingly severe. (Revelation 16:21)

In just two judgments, half of the world's population that's left after the rapture will die. In the first Scripture below, one-fourth of the earth perish by sword, famine, death, and wild animals. In the second, one-third of the people die.

> When he opened the fourth seal, I heard the fourth living creature saying, "Come and see!" And behold, a pale horse, and the name of he who sat on it was Death. Hades followed with

him. Authority over one fourth of the earth, to kill with the sword, with famine, with death, and by the wild animals of the earth was given to him. (Revelation 6:7-8)

The sixth angel sounded. I heard a voice from the horns of the golden altar which is before God, saying to the sixth angel who had the trumpet, "Free the four angels who are bound at the great river Euphrates!" The four angels were freed who had been prepared for that hour and day and month and year, so that they might kill one third of mankind. (Revelation 9:13-15)

These judgments have a couple purposes. No matter what happens, always remember that God loves you. He wants you to stop your wicked behavior and turn to him, turn to righteousness. See these terrible things as discipline from God. He's trying to get your attention and correct your life course. He's giving you a full display of his power so that you'll understand that he exists.

God did this in the past with judgments. Jonah was sent to tell Ninevah that God was going to overthrow them because of their wickedness. He was sent to preach God's word and call the people to repent. They did!

Yahweh's word came to Jonah the second time, saying, "Arise, go to Nineveh, that great city, and preach to it the message that I give you." ... Jonah began to enter into the city a day's journey, and he cried out, and said, "In forty days, Nineveh will be overthrown!" The people of Nineveh believed God.... The news reached the king of Nineveh.... He made a proclamation ... "Let neither man nor animal, herd nor flock, taste anything; let them not feed, nor drink water; but let them be covered with sackcloth, both man and animal, and let them cry mightily to God. Yes, let them turn everyone from his evil way, and from the violence that is in his hands. Who knows whether God will not turn and relent, and turn away from his fierce anger, so that we might not perish?" God saw their works, that they turned from their evil way. God relented of the disaster which he said he would do to them, and he didn't do it. (Jonah 3:1-2, 4-10)

We see in these verses that through judgments God wants people to hear of the wrath he intends to inflict on them. It's so they will turn from their evil, so God can forgive them.

In the fourth year of Jehoiakim the son of Josiah, king of Judah, this word came to Jeremiah from Yahweh, saying, "Take a scroll of a book, and write in it all the words that I have spoken to you against Israel, and against Judah, and against all the nations, from the day I spoke to you, from the days of Josiah, even to this day. It may be that the house of Judah will hear all the evil which I intend to do to them; that they may each return from his evil way; that I may forgive their iniquity and their sin." (Jeremiah 36:1-3)

He wants you to know who the one true God is. He's exposing the lies and false power of the Antichrist and Satan. There are millions of people like you seeking to understand the truth of the rapture and what's to come. I know you haven't hardened your heart toward God yet because you're still reading this book. God knows this too. This is your final warning from God. Time is running out. After these tribulation events, God will decide who gets to keep on living on earth in the millennial kingdom with Jesus. Only those who have put their faith in God and his son, Jesus, and his death for their sins will live in that kingdom.

Unfortunately, the Bible tells us that people will recognize the source of these judgments, but most will refuse to repent. These people will fully know that God is sending this terrible destruction and death, yet they continue to rebel against him. These are people who have made up their mind toward God. You see, they don't want anything to do with God. They don't want to live in heaven with God. They don't want to live on earth with Jesus. They want to continue doing wicked, evil things. They want to be like Satan. If you want to live like Satan, then God will let you. Then he will treat you just like he treats Satan. Satan is running amok on the planet right now deceiving you and helping you sin. These judgments are punishment for him and his followers.

These verses illustrate that the people know it's God because they see "him who sits on the throne." They know it's Jesus who is the "Lamb" sending these judgments to the earth, but they refuse to repent.

> The sky was removed like a scroll when it is rolled up. Every mountain and island was moved out of its place. The kings of the earth, the princes, the commanding officers, the rich, the strong, and every slave and free person, hid themselves in the caves and in the rocks of the mountains. They told the mountains and the rocks, "Fall on us, and hide us from the face of him who sits on the throne, and from the wrath of the Lamb, for the great day of his wrath has come; and who is able to stand?" (Revelation 6:14-17)

Even though they know it's coming from God, the people who aren't killed by the plagues still don't repent.

> The rest of mankind, who were not killed with these plagues, didn't repent of the works of their hands, that they wouldn't worship demons, and the idols of gold, and of silver, and of brass, and of stone, and of wood; which can't see, hear, or walk. They didn't repent of their murders, their sorceries, their sexual immorality, or their thefts. (Revelation 9:20-21)

In this verse, we see the people who survive the scorching sun don't repent. Instead, they blaspheme God. They know God is the one sending these judgments.

> People were scorched with great heat, and people blasphemed the name of God who has the power over these plagues. They didn't repent and give him glory. (Revelation 16:9)

I hope that you don't respond to God the way these people do. I hope that you choose to respond to God like Job did when trouble came upon him. When Satan came to ruin Job's life, at first Job got angry and envious of the wicked people who had it all and weren't being punished. But then Job encountered the mighty power of God and remembered his respect for God. Job then humbled himself before God and repented of his anger, bitterness, and prideful thoughts.

Here's Job's response to God. He knew God could do anything. Job was sorry and repented. Then he took back all the sinful things he said.

> Then Job answered Yahweh, "I know that you can do all things, and that no purpose of yours can be restrained. You asked, 'Who is this who hides counsel without knowledge?' therefore I have uttered that which I didn't understand, things too wonderful for me, which I didn't know. ... Therefore I abhor myself, and repent in dust and ashes." (Job 42:1-3, 6)

> I take back everything I said, and I sit in dust and ashes to show my repentance. (Job 42:6 NLT)

It's not too late for you, and it doesn't matter what you've done. God will forgive anything. He is bigger than your sin. God will forgive you. Take comfort in these verses.

> Therefore he is also able to save to the uttermost

those who draw near to God through him, seeing that he lives forever to make intercession for them. (Hebrews 7:25)

Seek Yahweh while he may be found. Call on him while he is near. Let the wicked forsake his way, and the unrighteous man his thoughts. Let him return to Yahweh, and he will have mercy on him, to our God, for he will freely pardon. (Isaiah 55:6-7)

19.4. The War Of Armageddon

Many people think Armageddon is synonymous with the end of the world. That's not the case. In actuality, this refers to a war that starts before the second coming of Jesus. This war occurs all across Israel and the place the Antichrist's army gathers is at *Armageddon*. The word itself means the hill of Megiddo. The city of Megiddo overlooks the valley of Jezreel in the great plain near Mount Carmel. This war is mainly between the Antichrist and God's chosen people, Israel. However, some leaders won't go along with what the Antichrist is doing. They'll rise up against him and destroy the city he reigns from. That city is referred to as Babylon in the Bible. That doesn't deter him from waging war against Israel though. Shortly after Jerusalem falls to the Antichrist, he turns his army against Jesus. The war ends when Jesus arrives at his second coming and vanquishes the enemy.

The war will center around Jerusalem in particular. The Antichrist will start this war when he breaks the peace treaty with Israel. Yes, he ends up breaking the peace treaty that he brokered. That's because it's a false peace treaty. His real motivation will be displayed for all to see. This happens three and a half years into the tribulation period. Remember those two witnesses preaching the gospel in Jerusalem? The Antichrist kills them while the entire world watches. Their bodies are left for all to see for several days before they are raised from the dead by

God. Then the Antichrist enters the Jewish temple. This will be their third temple, and it gets built during the tribulation period. When he enters the temple, he will declare himself God and commit an act that defiles the temple.

In these verses, we see the Antichrist goes to war against the two witnesses or "two prophets." The Antichrist is the "beast" and the "great city" is Jerusalem. It's because they were preaching the gospel, which is "their testimony," and tormenting the people on the earth with their signs and wonders.

> When they have finished their testimony, the beast that comes up out of the abyss will make war with them, and overcome them, and kill them. Their dead bodies will be in the street of the great city, which spiritually is called Sodom and Egypt, where also their Lord was crucified. From among the peoples, tribes, languages, and nations, people will look at their dead bodies for three and a half days, and will not allow their dead bodies to be laid in a tomb. Those who dwell on the earth rejoice over them, and they will be glad. They will give gifts to one another, because these two prophets tormented those who dwell on the earth. (Revelation 11:7-10)

At this same time, the Antichrist is going to overrun the Jewish temple and cause the offerings to stop. See Daniel 9:27 in Chapter 19.2. In this verse, "he" is the Antichrist.

We see in this Scripture that the Antichrist vents his anger against God's people. God's people are the people of the "holy covenant." The Antichrist is referred to as "the king of the North" and "he." Since he's against God's people, the Antichrist will show favor to all the unbelievers. Once he's desecrated the temple, he declares himself God.

> The king of the North will return to his own country with great wealth, but his heart will be set against the holy covenant. He will take action

against it and then return to his own country. At the appointed time he will invade the South again, but this time the outcome will be different from what it was before. Ships of the western coastlands will oppose him, and he will lose heart. Then he will turn back and vent his fury against the holy covenant. He will return and show favor to those who forsake the holy covenant. His armed forces will rise up to desecrate the temple fortress and will abolish the daily sacrifice. Then they will set up the abomination that causes desolation. ... The king will do as he pleases. He will exalt and magnify himself above every god and will say unheard-of things against the God of gods. (Daniel 11:28-31, 36 NIV)

The Antichrist then wages war against the Jewish people, forcing them to flee. Jesus, in the Scripture below, warned the people in Jerusalem to run to the mountains when the Antichrist invades the temple. It's so urgent, they shouldn't even go to their house to get stuff first because there would be oppression and unjust cruelty against them from the Antichrist.

"But when you see the abomination of desolation, spoken of by Daniel the prophet, standing where it ought not" (let the reader understand), "then let those who are in Judea flee to the mountains, and let him who is on the housetop not go down, nor enter in, to take anything out of his house. Let him who is in the field not return back to take his cloak. ... For in those days there will be oppression, such as there has not been the like from the beginning of the creation which God created until now, and never will be." (Mark 13:14-16, 19)

When the Antichrist wages this war, he brings all nations against Jerusalem. These verses tell us the city will be plundered, and women will be raped. Of the inhabitants who didn't escape, half are captured, and the other half are left among the ruins.

Behold, a day of Yahweh comes, when your plunder will be divided within you. For I will gather all nations against Jerusalem to battle; and the city will be taken, the houses rifled, and the women ravished. Half of the city will go out into captivity, and the rest of the people will not be cut off from the city. (Zechariah 14:1-2)

It's not just Jerusalem that falls at the hands of the Antichrist. These verses illustrate that "he" invades many countries. The "king of the North" is a reference to the Antichrist. The "beautiful land" refers to Israel.

At the time of the end the king of the South will engage him in battle, and the king of the North will storm out against him with chariots and cavalry and a great fleet of ships. He will invade many countries and sweep through them like a flood. He will also invade the Beautiful Land. Many countries will fall, but Edom, Moab and the leaders of Ammon will be delivered from his hand. (Daniel 11:40-41 NIV)

A great many people participate in this war in the Antichrist's army. 200 million! There's a rather curious description in the Bible about this army. Let's read it.

Saying to the sixth angel who had the trumpet, "Free the four angels who are bound at the great river Euphrates!" The four angels were freed who had been prepared for that hour and day and month and year, so that they might kill one third of mankind. The number of the armies of the horsemen was two hundred million. I heard the number of them. Thus I saw the horses in the vision, and those who sat on them, having breastplates of fiery red, hyacinth blue, and sulfur yellow; and the horses' heads resembled lions' heads. Out of their mouths proceed fire, smoke, and sulfur. (Revelation 9:14-17)

The way the army is described, it seems to be a demonic army of fallen angels. Look at the horses they're riding. I've never seen a horse with a head like a lion's that can breathe fire and sulfur. Normal horses don't look like that or do that. No, breathing fire is what dragons do. And who do we know is the dragon? That's Satan.

In addition to the demonic army, we see in this Scripture that the fallen angels convince kings of the entire earth to gather for battle at Armageddon. Remember that the "beast" is the Antichrist. These verses are also where we learn the army gathers in the place called Armageddon.

> The sixth angel poured out his bowl on the great river Euphrates, and its water was dried up to prepare the way for the kings from the East. Then I saw three impure spirits that looked like frogs; they came out of the mouth of the dragon, out of the mouth of the beast and out of the mouth of the false prophet. They are demonic spirits that perform signs, and they go out to the kings of the whole world, to gather them for the battle on the great day of God Almighty. ... Then they gathered the kings together to the place that in Hebrew is called Armageddon. (Revelation 16:12-14, 16 NIV)

The number who gather to wage war here is hard to fathom. We've got the demonic army of 200 million. Then we've got the armies of kings from all over the earth as well. So it's probably more like 400 million who are gathered. Now let that number of soldiers sink in for a moment. In July 2019, the United States population was estimated at 329 million.[30] That volume of demonic soldiers alone is 60 percent of the United States population!

Why have that many gathered for war? Did you notice the demons gathered all of them at Armageddon? It's because Jesus is coming! The demons know when to expect him. I've told you that you can know the day he'll return as well. You see, they've turned the war raging against God's people to a war against God himself.

At Jesus's second coming we see the Antichrist, who is the "beast," the kings of the earth, and their armies gathered to war against Jesus and his army of believers from heaven. In this Scripture, Jesus is the one called "Faithful and True."

> I saw the heaven opened, and behold, a white horse, and he who sat on it is called Faithful and True. In righteousness he judges and makes war. His eyes are a flame of fire, and on his head are many crowns. ... He is clothed in a garment sprinkled with blood. His name is called "The Word of God." The armies which are in heaven followed him on white horses, clothed in white, pure, fine linen. ... I saw the beast, and the kings of the earth, and their armies, gathered together to make war against him who sat on the horse, and against his army. (Revelation 19:11-14, 19)

19.5. Jesus Returns

Jesus is coming back to earth at the end of the seven year tribulation period, during the war of Armageddon. This is referred to as the second coming of Jesus. When he comes back a whole bunch of things take place. Let's look at what happens.

Jesus will come back in a spectacular display of power and glory. The Bible tells us he returns the same way he left, in the clouds. He'll come on the clouds to the Mount of Olives, "Olivet," in Jerusalem. When his feet touch earth, a great earthquake will split the mountain. In this Scripture, Jesus is "he" who "was taken up."

> When he had said these things, as they were looking, he was taken up, and a cloud received him out of their sight. While they were looking steadfastly into the sky as he went, behold, two men stood by them in white clothing, who also said, "You men of Galilee, why do you stand

> looking into the sky? This Jesus, who was received up from you into the sky, will come back in the same way as you saw him going into the sky." Then they returned to Jerusalem from the mountain called Olivet, which is near Jerusalem, a Sabbath day's journey away. (Acts 1:9-12)

The Mount of Olives is the mountain just east of Jerusalem. When Jesus returns, there will be an earthquake that splits the mountain. It'll move north and south, creating a large valley.

> Then Yahweh will go out and fight against those nations, as when he fought in the day of battle. His feet will stand in that day on the Mount of Olives, which is before Jerusalem on the east; and the Mount of Olives will be split in two, from east to west, making a very great valley. Half of the mountain will move toward the north, and half of it toward the south. (Zechariah 14:3-4)

Jesus will not be alone when he returns. All those people who were raptured and who were resurrected at the rapture are with him! In these verses, they are depicted as the "saints" and the "armies which are in heaven."

> It was given to her that she would array herself in bright, pure, fine linen: for the fine linen is the righteous acts of the saints. ... The armies which are in heaven followed him on white horses, clothed in white, pure, fine linen. (Revelation 19:8, 14)

Here's something else spectacular about Jesus's return. Everyone will see it! I'm not going to guess how God is going to do this, but it's going to be epic. When he comes on the clouds every single eye will see him.

> Jesus Christ, the faithful witness, the firstborn of the dead, and the ruler of the kings of the earth. To

him who loves us, and washed us from our sins by his blood.... ... Behold, he is coming with the clouds, and every eye will see him, including those who pierced him. All the tribes of the earth will mourn over him. Even so, Amen. (Revelation 1:5, 7)

When Jesus returns the world is at war. The first thing he does is stop the war at Armageddon. Jesus throws the Antichrist, who is the "beast," and False Prophet into the lake of fire, hell. Then Jesus kills everyone else who gathered against him in that war. He does it by speaking. That's the "sword which came out of his mouth." Once again, Jesus is the one called "Faithful and True" and the "Word of God."

> I saw the heaven opened, and behold, a white horse, and he who sat on it is called Faithful and True. In righteousness he judges and makes war. His eyes are a flame of fire, and on his head are many crowns. ... He is clothed in a garment sprinkled with blood. His name is called "The Word of God." ... Out of his mouth proceeds a sharp, double-edged sword, that with it he should strike the nations. ... He has on his garment and on his thigh a name written, "KING OF KINGS, AND LORD OF LORDS." ... I saw the beast, and the kings of the earth, and their armies, gathered together to make war against him who sat on the horse, and against his army. The beast was taken, and with him the false prophet.... These two were thrown alive into the lake of fire that burns with sulfur. The rest were killed with the sword of him who sat on the horse, the sword which came out of his mouth. (Revelation 19:11-13, 15-16, 19-21)

After Jesus defeats the Antichrist, then he binds Satan for 1,000 years. In these verses, the "dragon" is Satan.

> I saw an angel coming down out of heaven, having the key of the abyss and a great chain in his hand. He seized the dragon, the old serpent, which is the devil and Satan, who deceives the whole inhabited earth, and bound him for a thousand years, and cast him into the abyss, and shut it, and sealed it over him, that he should deceive the nations no more, until the thousand years were finished. After this, he must be freed for a short time. (Revelation 20:1-3)

Jesus will then separate the believers, who are the "sheep," from the unbelievers, who are the "goats." Believers get to enter Jesus's kingdom on earth. Unbelievers are sent to the "eternal fire," hell. In this Scripture, Jesus is the "Son of Man."

> But when the Son of Man comes in his glory, and all the holy angels with him, then he will sit on the throne of his glory. Before him all the nations will be gathered, and he will separate them one from another, as a shepherd separates the sheep from the goats. He will set the sheep on his right hand, but the goats on the left. Then the King will tell those on his right hand, "Come, blessed of my Father, inherit the Kingdom prepared for you from the foundation of the world...." ... Then he will say also to those on the left hand, "Depart from me, you cursed, into the eternal fire which is prepared for the devil and his angels." (Matthew 25:31-34, 41)

The great news about Jesus's return is that everyone who has put their faith in Jesus during the tribulation gets to live with Jesus now. The Bible tells us that Jesus will reign from Jerusalem. He's going to have a lot of helpers reigning with him. All the people who were raptured or resurrected at the rapture are among those who will rule across the earth. In this Scripture, they are the ones sitting on thrones.

> I saw thrones, and they sat on them, and

judgment was given to them. I saw the souls of those who had been beheaded for the testimony of Jesus, and for the word of God, and such as didn't worship the beast nor his image, and didn't receive the mark on their forehead and on their hand. They lived and reigned with Christ for a thousand years. The rest of the dead didn't live until the thousand years were finished. This is the first resurrection. Blessed and holy is he who has part in the first resurrection. Over these, the second death has no power, but they will be priests of God and of Christ, and will reign with him one thousand years. (Revelation 20:4-6)

That's not it though. Jesus also resurrects the bodies of all the Old Testament believers and the people who died during the tribulation. In the verses above, the "souls of those who had been beheaded" for Jesus refers to the tribulation saints. They get glorified bodies now as well. This Scripture below tells us that Michael, an angel, will be fighting against Satan during the war. After Jesus rescues his people, many "who sleep" will awake to "everlasting life." These are the Old Testament believers who get new bodies now too (see also Psalm 50:1-6).

At that time Michael will stand up, the great prince who stands for the children of your people; and there will be a time of trouble, such as never was since there was a nation even to that same time. At that time your people will be delivered, everyone who is found written in the book. Many of those who sleep in the dust of the earth will awake, some to everlasting life, and some to shame and everlasting contempt. ... But you, Daniel, shut up the words, and seal the book, even to the time of the end. ... But go your way until the end; for you will rest, and will stand in your inheritance at the end of the days. (Daniel 12:1-2, 4, 13)

If you are left behind, have put your faith in Jesus,

and you're alive at Jesus second coming, those people will be living in Jesus's kingdom on earth with you. You'll be living on earth with Jesus and among immortals. How "cool" and awesome is this!

Lastly, Jesus will establish his kingdom on earth and reign for 1,000 years. This kingdom begins with just believers. Remember that Jesus isn't the only one who returns at his second coming. Jesus brings everyone who was in heaven with him. That's the Old Testament believers and tribulation saints. He also brings people who were raptured and believers resurrected at the rapture. Those now immortal believers will reign with Jesus in his earthly kingdom.

Let the coming reign of Jesus bring you comfort and peace. If you've put your faith in Jesus, what you are experiencing right now on earth is as bad as life will ever get for you. These verses tell us that Jesus's reign will be a time of unparalleled peace and prosperity on earth. "He" is a reference to Jesus, and "they" refers to the people living in the millennial kingdom.

> I will rejoice in Jerusalem, and delight in my people; and the voice of weeping and the voice of crying will be heard in her no more. (Isaiah 65:19)

> He will judge between the nations, and will decide concerning many peoples. They shall beat their swords into plowshares, and their spears into pruning hooks. Nation shall not lift up sword against nation, neither shall they learn war any more. (Isaiah 2:4)

The apostle Paul tells us when Jesus appears, God will provide rest for those who are left behind who are being persecuted for their faith in Jesus. You're going to be praising him on that day. You'll be bringing him glory because you believed.

> And God will provide rest for you who are being persecuted and also for us when the Lord Jesus

appears from heaven. He will come with his mighty angels, in flaming fire, bringing judgment on those who don't know God and on those who refuse to obey the Good News of our Lord Jesus. They will be punished with eternal destruction, forever separated from the Lord and from his glorious power. When he comes on that day, he will receive glory from his holy people—praise from all who believe. And this includes you, for you believed what we told you about him. So we keep on praying for you, asking our God to enable you to live a life worthy of his call. May he give you the power to accomplish all the good things your faith prompts you to do. (2 Thessalonians 1:7-11 NLT)

Part 8
What To Do If
You're Left Behind

Chapter 20 - Left Behind Complete Checklist

Here's a simple checklist of what you need to do if you're left behind. These items focus on both your spiritual survival and your physical survival.

1. Make a decision about Jesus

I'm hoping you've already checked the box on this item. After all you've read and learned in this book, you are fully equipped to make a decision about your eternal future. This is truly the most important decision you need to make. That's why it's first on the list. Do you choose to believe that Jesus Christ died for your sins to give you eternal life?

2. Pray to accept Jesus

If you've decided to believe, then congratulations are in order! Heaven is rejoicing. All you need to do is tell God the decision you've made to believe. You can pray something like this.

"Dear Lord Jesus,

I know that I'm a sinner. Please forgive me of my sins. I believe that you are the son of God and that you died for my sins. I also believe that you rose from the grave and are reigning in heaven with God. I want to turn from my sins and follow you as Lord and Savior. Please help me by coming into my heart and life. Thank you for making a way for me to live with you in heaven for eternity. In Jesus's name, amen."

3. Get a Bible

In order for you to have a relationship with Jesus, you need to know Jesus. The Bible is Jesus. He's the Word of God. He's written on every page. I recommend you get multiple formats of the Bible. Don't rely on being able to use a Bible app or online Bible website. I'm sure those will get removed over time as the Antichrist's power increases and hatred against Christianity rises. Have digital copies that are pdf, doc, or text files that you can open in common applications. Have an audio version you can listen to. Have some physical copies in paperback. I also recommend that you get multiple translations of the Bible. That will help you learn the Scripture better. Perhaps start with the World English Bible that's in the public domain and free. It's more of a word for word translation. You can find links to download it in many formats on my website, rapture911.com. Then get yourself a translation like the New Living Translation that's really easy to read and understand.

4. Gather Bible resources

It's important to study the Word of God. You'll need some resources to do this effectively. Get a Bible commentary and a Bible concordance. While you can use online resources and apps for these, don't rely on those being around and accessible for you. I recommend you get a paperback book or download the eBook versions. Matthew Henry wrote a Bible commentary in 1706 that contains a comprehensive exposition of every verse in the Bible.[31] It's a standard resource still used today and it's in the public domain, so it's free to read and use as you wish. It's not written in old English, so it's easy to read. James Strong wrote a concordance in 1890 that indexed every word in the King James Version of the Bible.[32] So if you want to read every verse about love, this would tell you all the verses to read. It's still the standard concordance used today. It's also in the public domain and free to read and use. I have links to download them on my website, rapture911.com.

Also stock up on Bible study books. Get these while they are still available. Also download or purchase sermons and teachings from respected pastors and Bible teachers. Record, download, or purchase teachings broadcast on the Christian television networks too. These will likely only be available online for a short period of time. Go to the Wayback Machine website at archive.org/web/ to view archived pages of websites.33 Learn how to archive a website for offline viewing. You can do an Internet search and find instructions and software that will help you. Get what you can while you can.

5. Store up food for your soul

It's also important to consume information and content that's good for you. Make sure you have some good music to listen to that's not full of sinful lyrics. You want content that helps you think of things above. Things that are heavenly or godly. Consider Christian, gospel, classical, instrumental, and jazz music. Also think about getting some books, movies, and TV shows that are good for your soul as well. Remember that the content that has a Christian message will likely not be available long, so look for it now.

6. Get physical survival resources

It's not going to be easy to survive through or even live during the tribulation period. You should expect there will be times that you will not have the items you take for granted today, like electricity, running water, and gas for heating and cooking. You should be prepared to survive without those things. I recommend you get these types of books: survival basics, first aid, and prepping. Those resources will teach you what to do.

7. Pack an emergency "bug out" bag

You'll want to pack a bag that contains some basic survival gear that's ready when an emergency happens. Then you just need to grab the bag and take it if you need to evacuate, "bug out," or leave your house very quickly for an emergency. The survival book you get should tell you what to include in this. You can also do an Internet search and find all sorts of checklists and suggestions of what to include. The next few items on this checklist will give you some ideas on where to start.

8. Be able to filter water

Water is key to your physical survival. You won't live more than a few days without it. When an emergency strikes you may not have access to clean drinking water. Make sure you have a way to filter water. The water filter you have on your faucet sink will not cut it for this. I'm talking about having the ability to put muddy river water into a filter and getting clean drinking water out. There are all sorts of devices available that you can get. Keep this with your "bug out" bag along with a water bottle.

9. Have a temporary shelter

Many times you will not be able to stay in your home during an emergency. You should have something you can use to provide temporary shelter for yourself. A camping tent or even some tarps will come in handy. Consider getting a sleeping bag too.

10. Stock up on food

During an emergency you likely won't have the ability to cook food in your microwave, on your stove, or in your oven. You'll need an off the grid cooking solution, like a fire pit or grill. Along with that you'll need fuel and a fire starter. Consider having a supply of food that doesn't require cooking that you can use during an emergency. The book I recommended you get on prepping will help you do this. Have some canned foods handy, along with a can opener. Unprocessed and not ground grains keep long term, like oatmeal as rolled oats (not instant), white rice, pasta, and popcorn. Beans are a good source of nutrition and also keep well long term. Salt, sugar, honey, and pure maple syrup are good items to have on hand as well. Put these items in mylar bags to protect them from moisture and bugs and store them inside big, five-gallon, plastic buckets. Make sure you have a hand crank grain mill. Otherwise, when the power goes out you could be grinding grain with a stone like our ancient ancestors did.

11. Build a first aid kit

Make sure you have a basic first aid kit available and in your "bug out" bag. Be sure you include items that are specific to your individual needs, like medications you need. Also think about natural disinfectants you could use in time of need. Salt, vinegar, and aloe are good natural remedies when used properly. The first aid book I recommended you get will help you build a proper kit.

12. Put some clothing in your "bug out" bag

Make sure you include some basic clothing items in your "bug out" bag. You may need to leave in the middle of the night when you aren't properly dressed. Include items to protect you from the sun, rain, and cold.

13. Get some survival tools and gear

A good knife is a must for your "bug out" bag. You'll be able to use it for all sorts of things. You should also consider including tools and gear like a mini shovel, multi-purpose tool, folding saw, duct tape, para cord, a small mirror, a whistle, a hand crank radio, a compass, some solar lights, a solar charger, and a mask for air filtration. Don't forget about sanitation supplies like a bucket and a garbage bag. You may need to hunt or fish, so make sure you have gear for that. Lastly, consider that you may need to protect yourself from animals or people. Pepper spray, a big stick, or a taser will go a long way. Of course, you could include a more sophisticated weapon, like a gun, if you're adequately trained and prepared to use it and also store it safely.

14. Learn to barter

You learned in this book that the global ruler, the Antichrist, will establish a new economic and monetary system. Participation in that system will require allegiance to the Antichrist, who you know is indwelt by Satan. If you've put your faith in Jesus, and you want to enter heaven, then you can't have any part of that system. You're not going to be able to buy or sell anything very easily. So you need to be prepared to barter with others. Bartering is just trading something you have for something you need or want. You can trade goods, a skill, a service, or labor. God has blessed you with many abilities and skills. Think of how you could bless other people with your God-given abilities in exchange for something else. Consider learning a trade skill that could come in handy, something like carpentry, sewing, or farming.

15. Join a community

I'm sure many of you think you'd easily be able to live off of the land during an emergency. You've watched apocalypse shows and movies and seen how it's done after all. The honest truth is that's a fantasy for most of you reading this. It requires a great deal of specialized skills, mental acuity, and physical fitness. Do not count on being able to survive on your own. You will need a community of people to have the best chance of success. In a community, you'll have a variety of skill sets and knowledge to tap into. Two heads really are better than one when it comes to problem solving. The other benefit of community is protection. You already know there is safety in numbers. A community will also provide the emotional support that you'll need during this time.

A community doesn't necessarily mean a communal home that everyone lives in together. It could be as simple as having a real relationship with all the neighbors in your community. Having regular neighborhood meetings, Bible classes, bartering events, survival lessons, etc.

16. Don't worry about those who vanished

I know you're concerned about the people who vanished. You don't need to be. The people who vanished put their faith in Jesus Christ. They were taken to heaven where they safely reside. If you've put your faith in Jesus, you'll see them again. Remember that they'll be with Jesus at his second coming. If you don't survive through the tribulation, then you'll see them in heaven.

17. Bless others

After Jesus gets a hold of you, you'll never be the same. You'll wish you had known him sooner. You'll start to see everything he's done for you and how much he loves you. You'll start to become more loving and more giving. You'll want to bless others because he's blessed you. These Scriptures tell us that when we help and bless others, we're actually helping and blessing Jesus. These are sacrifices that please God.

> Then the righteous will answer him, saying, "Lord, when did we see you hungry and feed you, or thirsty and give you a drink? When did we see you as a stranger and take you in, or naked and clothe you? When did we see you sick or in prison and come to you?" The King will answer them, "Most certainly I tell you, because you did it to one of the least of these my brothers, you did it to me." (Matthew 25:37-40)

> But don't forget to be doing good and sharing, for with such sacrifices God is well pleased. (Hebrews 13:16)

18. Save a life

Don't keep your faith in Jesus a secret! Go tell someone. You just might save their life.

> Brothers, if any among you wanders from the truth and someone turns him back, let him know that he who turns a sinner from the error of his way will save a soul from death and will cover a multitude of sins. (James 5:19-20)

19. Get to know Jesus

While you're waiting for Jesus to return, get to know Jesus. If you've put your faith in him, then you'll be spending eternity with him. Getting to know him will bring you comfort and peace during this troubling time. It will also delight Jesus and give you something to be truly proud about.

> Yahweh says, "Don't let the wise man glory in his wisdom. Don't let the mighty man glory in his might. Don't let the rich man glory in his riches. But let him who glories glory in this, that he has understanding, and knows me, that I am Yahweh who exercises loving kindness, justice, and righteousness in the earth, for I delight in these things," says Yahweh. (Jeremiah 9:23-24)

This Scripture states that Jesus will bring you peace and comfort when you have a relationship with him. Keep reading the Bible and praying.

> In nothing be anxious, but in everything, by prayer and petition with thanksgiving, let your requests be made known to God. And the peace of God, which surpasses all understanding, will guard your hearts and your thoughts in Christ Jesus. (Philippians 4:6-7)

20. Be watching for Jesus's return

No matter what happens on earth during this battle between good and evil, know that Jesus has already won. Jesus conquered Satan when he died on the cross and rose from the dead. Jesus is coming again. You will reap the promises he's given you.

Jesus said people would lack courage because of things happening on the earth but to lift your head and keep your eyes on him because your redemption is coming soon.

> There will be signs in the sun, moon, and stars; and on the earth anxiety of nations, in perplexity for the roaring of the sea and the waves; men fainting for fear, and for expectation of the things which are coming on the world: for the powers of the heavens will be shaken. Then they will see the Son of Man coming in a cloud with power and

> great glory. But when these things begin to happen, look up and lift up your heads, because your redemption is near. (Luke 21:25-28)

Jesus is coming, and he's bringing rewards with him.

> Behold, I come quickly. My reward is with me, to repay to each man according to his work. I am the Alpha and the Omega, the First and the Last, the Beginning and the End. … I, Jesus, have sent my angel to testify these things to you for the assemblies. I am the root and the offspring of David, the Bright and Morning Star. (Revelation 22:12-13, 16)

If you've put your faith in Jesus, you can overcome being left behind because Jesus has overcome.

> Jesus answered them … "I have told you these things, that in me you may have peace. In the world you have trouble; but cheer up! I have overcome the world." (John 16:31, 33)

Final Thoughts

It's been a pleasure helping you learn about God and Jesus, lies you'll encounter from the enemy, and what's to come. I pray that you've come to realize you can trust Jesus with your life. He loves you so much that he died for you. Let him love you for all eternity and lavish you with all the promises he's revealed in his word.

As a believer left behind, be strong, courageous, and bold in your faith. The power of Jesus Christ lives inside of you. He overcame every force of evil against him. Because he overcame and conquered death, he will give you the strength to do likewise and accomplish his purpose for you.

If I don't see you in heaven before Jesus's second coming, you know where to find me. I'll be on a white horse coming on the clouds with him. What a marvelous day it will be! See you then.

Thanks for taking this journey with me. If you'd like to show your support for my work, please leave a review wherever you purchased this book. It's free to do, and it'll only take you a minute to write a quick sentence expressing your thoughts about the book. Your review is very important to independent, self-published authors like me. Internet and online bookstore algorithms favor books with reviews. They display in search results and at the top of search results more often than books without reviews. I even need a minimum number of reviews before I can purchase certain advertising. So, your review will help more people find this book. That will in turn help me sell more books, which means I can keep writing books for you. Go to rapture911.com/reviews if you need a link to where you can leave a review.

Thanks for your support!

Marsha

Want More Truth?
Read the Full Edition

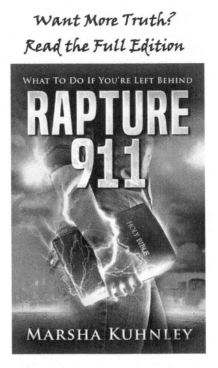

The full edition of *Rapture 911: What To Do If You're Left Behind* includes:

- Additional information about the rapture and why it happened.
- More lies exposed so you won't be deceived.
- Examples of prophecies fulfilled that prove God's Word is trustworthy.
- Coping mechanisms from Biblical heroes to better handle shame, grief, and fear.
- Extra content to help you build your faith and be good to your soul.
- Complete timeline of future events.
- A handy Bible glossary.

Get FREE Books

Rapture911.com/free

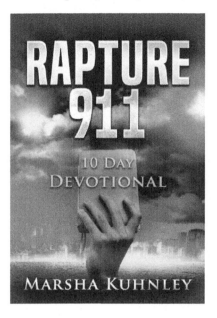

Books By Marsha Kuhnley

Rapture 911 Series
*Rapture 911: What To Do If You're Left Behind

Rapture 911: What To Do If You're Left Behind
(Pocket Edition)

Rapture 911: 10 Day Devotional

Rapture 911: Prophecy Reference Bible

End Times Armor Series
The Election Omen: Your Vote Matters

The Election Omen: 10 Day Devotional

Other Works
Seeing The Light In Dark Times: 10 Day Devotional

Visit Marsha's website to find these books
rapture911.com

* - Also available as an audiobook

About The Author

Marsha Kuhnley is an American author of Christian non-fiction books. She has a passion for Bible prophecy, finance, and economics. She received her MBA in Finance and BA in Economics from the University of New Mexico. Prior to becoming an author, she enjoyed a career at Intel Corporation. She uses her education and career experience to take complex Biblical information and present it in easily understandable concepts. You'll benefit from over a decade of her research and study of the Bible, Bible prophecy, and Rapture theology. She lives in Albuquerque, NM with her husband where they attend Calvary Church.

Connect With Marsha

rapture911.com/connect

Endnotes

1 Dr. C. Truman Davis, "A Physician's View Of The Crucifixion Of Jesus Christ," CBN, https://www1.cbn.com/medical-view-of-the-crucifixion-of-jesus-christ, accessed September 7, 2019.

2 "Roman Legion," Wikipedia, https://en.wikipedia.org/wiki/Roman_legion, accessed September 7, 2019.

3 Gary Bates and Lita Cosner, "UFOlogy: The World's Fastest-Growing 'Scientific' Religion?," *Creation.com*, May 12, 2011, https://creation.com/ufology-scientific-religion, accessed September 7, 2019.

4 David Wallace-Wells, James D. Walsh, Neel Patel, Clint Rainey, Katie Heaney, Eric Benson, and Tim Urban, "Reasons To Believe: How Seriously Should You Take Those Recent Reports of UFOs? Ask The Pentagon. Or Read This Primer For The SETI-Curious.," *Intelligencer*, March 20, 2018, http://nymag.com/intelligencer/2018/03/13-reasons-to-believe-aliens-are-real.html, accessed September 7, 2019.

5 Billy Crone, https://www.getalifemedia.com/, accessed September 7, 2019.

6 "UFO's: The Great Last Days Deception," Get A Life Ministries, https://www.getalifemedia.com/video/apologetics/ufo.shtml, accessed September 7, 2019. Video 10 - A Condensed Study of UFO's.

7 "UFO's: The Great Last Days Deception," Get A Life Ministries, https://www.getalifemedia.com/video/apologetics/ufo.shtml, accessed September 7, 2019. Video 10 - A Condensed Study of UFO's.

8 "The CE4 Research Group," CE4 Research Group, http://www.alienresistance.org/ce4.htm, accessed September 7, 2019.

9 "All Time Box Office: Domestic Grosses Adjusted For Ticket Price Inflation," Box Office Mojo, https://www.boxofficemojo.com/alltime/adjusted.htm, accessed August 14, 2019.

10 "Storm Area 51, They Can't Stop All of Us"," Facebook Public Event, September 20, 2019,

https://www.facebook.com/events/extraterrestrial-highway-area-51/storm-area-51-they-cant-stop-all-of-us/448435052621047/, accessed August 7, 2019.

[11] "List Of Metropolitan Statistical Areas," Wikipedia, https://en.wikipedia.org/wiki/List_of_metropolitan_statistical_areas#United_States, accessed September 7, 2019. United States data.

[12] Greg, "Jacques Vallee - On Messengers Of Deception," *Daily Grail*, July 17, 2008, https://www.dailygrail.com/2008/07/jacques-vallee-on-messengers-of-deception/, accessed September 7, 2019.

[13] Gary Bates, "UFOs Are Not Extraterrestrial!," *Creation.com*, July 5, 2016, https://creation.com/ufos-not-extraterrestrial, accessed September 7, 2019.

[14] Kimberly Hickok, "China's New Laser Gun Can Zap You With A Silent, Carbonizing Beam," *Live Science*, July 2, 2018, https://www.livescience.com/62973-china-laser-guns.html, accessed September 7, 2019.

[15] Andrew Liptak, "The US Air Force Successfully Tested A Laser System To Shoot Down Missiles," *The Verge*, May 5, 2019, https://www.theverge.com/2019/5/5/18530089/us-air-force-research-laboratory-shield-laser-weapons-system-test, accessed September 7, 2019.

[16] Donovan Alexander, "Colonizing The Moon Could Be The Key To Saving The Earth, Says Jeff Bezos," *Interesting Engineering*, June 9, 2019, https://interestingengineering.com/colonizing-the-moon-could-be-the-key-to-saving-the-earth-says-jeff-bezos, accessed September 7, 2019.

[17] Drew Scherban, "Beam Me Up Scotty! Researchers Teleport Particle Of Light Six Kilometres," *University of Calgary*, August 20, 2016, https://www.ucalgary.ca/news/beam-me-scotty-researchers-teleport-particle-light-six-kilometres, accessed September 7, 2019.

[18] Corey S. Powell, "Elon Musk Says We May Live In A Simulation. Here's How We Might Tell If He's Right," *NBC News*, October 2, 2018, https://www.nbcnews.com/mach/science/what-simulation-hypothesis-why-some-think-life-simulated-reality-ncna913926, accessed September 7, 2019.

[19] Nick Statt, "Comma.ai Founder George Hotz Wants To Free Humanity From The AI Simulation," *The Verge*,

March 9, 2019,
https://www.theverge.com/2019/3/9/18258030/george-hotz-ai-simulation-jailbreaking-reality-sxsw-2019, accessed September 7, 2019.

[20] Dan Vergano, "It's Starting To Look Like God Won't Save Us From Global Warming," *BuzzFeed News*, April 24, 2019,
https://www.buzzfeednews.com/article/danvergano/pope-didnt-fix-climate-change, accessed September 7, 2019.

[21] Kim Stanley Robinson, "Empty Half The Earth Of It's Humans. It's The Only Way To Save The Planet," *The Guardian*, March 20, 2018,
https://www.theguardian.com/cities/2018/mar/20/save-the-planet-half-earth-kim-stanley-robinson, accessed September 7, 2019.

[22] Klint Finley and Gregory Barber, "The WIRED Guide To The Blockchain," *Wired*, July 9, 2019,
https://www.wired.com/story/guide-blockchain/, accessed September 7, 2019.

[23] Sue Halpern, "Facebook's Audacious Pitch For A Global Cryptocurrency," *The New Yorker*, July 30, 2019,
https://www.newyorker.com/tech/annals-of-technology/facebooks-audacious-pitch-for-a-global-cryptocurrency, accessed September 7, 2019.

[24] Noelle Acheson, "Bitcoin Won't Be a Global Reserve Currency. But It's Opening The Box," *Coindesk*, August 3, 2019, https://www.coindesk.com/bitcoin-wont-be-a-global-reserve-currency-but-its-opening-the-box, accessed September 7, 2019.

[25] "Stats," Facebook.com,
https://newsroom.fb.com/company-info/, accessed September 7, 2019.

[26] "About Us," Walmart.com,
https://corporate.walmart.com/our-story, accessed September 7, 2019.

[27] Steve Warren and Benjamin Gill, "Elon Musk Wants To Chip Your Brain: Is Biohacking About Convenience Or A Shift To The Mark Of The Beast?," *CBN News*, July 17, 2019,
https://www1.cbn.com/cbnnews/2019/july/biohacking-technological-convenience-or-shift-to-revelations-mark-of-the-beast, accessed September 7, 2019.

[28] Bailey Reutzel, "I Got The Mark Of The Beast-And It Will Hold My Bitcoin," *Coindesk*, March 15, 2019, https://www.coindesk.com/i-got-the-mark-of-the-beast-and-itll-hold-my-bitcoin, accessed September 7, 2019.

[29] Skip Heitzig, *You Can Understand the Book of Revelation*, (Harvest House Publishers, 2011), Chapter 13.

[30] "U.S. And World Population Clock," United States Census Bureau, https://www.census.gov/popclock/, accessed July 19, 2019.

[31] Matthew Henry, *Matthew Henry's Commentary on the Whole Bible*, (n.p.: 1706-1720), https://www.blueletterbible.org/commentaries/mhc/, accessed September 10, 2019.

[32] James Strong, *The Exhaustive Concordance Of The Bible*, (New York, NY: Eaton & Mains, 1890), https://archive.org/stream/exhaustiveconcor1890stro#page/n11/mode/2up, accessed September 10, 2019.

[33] Internet Archive Wayback Machine, archive.org/web/, accessed September 10, 2019.